QUESTIONS FOR JESUS

CONVERSATIONAL PRAYER AROUND YOUR DEEPEST DESIRES

TONY STOLTZFUS

WITH KATHY STOLTZFUS AND SARA HERRING

Published by Coach22 Bookstore LLC
15618 Mule Mountain Parkway, Redding, CA. 96001
www.Coach22.com

ISBN-10: 1492177350
ISBN-13: 978-1492177357

Cover Design by Tony Stoltzfus
Interior Design and formatting by Lorraine Box

Some of the anecdotal illustrations in this book are true to life, and are included with the permission of the persons involved. All other illustrations are composites where names and details have been changed. Any resemblance to persons living or dead is coincidental.

TABLE OF
CONTENTS

QUESTIONS
FOR JESUS

Most of us as grew up learning to pray about the business of being a Christian.

We ask for help to do the right thing, pray that our relatives will know God, or petition him to bless what we are doing for him. We ask forgiveness (at best) or grovel (at worst) about the things we do wrong, and return repeatedly for direction and confirmation so we're certain we know what we're supposed to do.

My times with God used to sound like that. Morning devotions felt like work—which is no surprise, because that's what my prayers were about: work. Almost all of them contained the word "do"—as in, 'What do you want me to do?' or 'I did this wrong, I'm sorry' or 'Help me do better.' It was a hard slog, this difficult business of living the Christian life. Yet God was laughing—laughing!—because he saw his secret plan to revolutionize my business-oriented prayer life coming to fruition.

When he was finished (I'm a slow learner—it took 20 years), I'd discovered how to talk to Jesus about the relationship instead of just the business. And that changed everything. Now we mostly talk about what we like about each other, what we're thinking and feeling, and our future in heaven; and a lot less about my next assignment and past mistakes. I like that.

So how did he teach me to pray? I'll save the painful part where he tore down my existing devotional life for later, and skip to when I started to tune into something new. One key moment was when I asked him what to do in a challenging coaching session. "Jesus, I'm not sure what approach to take with this person. What do you want me to do?" It was one of those, 'Oh-Jesus-I-feel-inadequate-please-please-help-me prayers'. But his reply surprised me: "Why are you asking me? I like watching you function."

Wait a minute—he enjoys letting me decide and watching me be who I am? What about God's will and all that? A big old chunk of my paradigm of relating with God was that you talk to God so he can tell you what you are supposed to do. This hinted at something really different—what was I missing?

The image I needed to grasp from what he was saying had already been planted in my life by a decade-long career as a life coach. From years of experience, I absolutely knew that asking was more powerful than telling, and that believing in someone's ability to think for themselves produced more change and better results than giving them advice. I was totally committed to not being a teller. But could it be that I'd spent my life trying to get God to be a teller for me, and that wasn't his style at all?

Another important moment came during a three-month sabbatical where I'd cut back to one day a week of work and six days of Sabbath. It was much more of a struggle to embrace the rhythm of rest than I'd anticipated. In the process, I discovered that many of the behaviors I wrestled with in life grew out of a deep desire for inner peace.

My image of peace was summer vacation as a kid: endless days outdoors under a blue sky, lying on the green grass watching the shapes in the clouds, with never a deadline or to-do or responsibility to interrupt my bliss. Aaaah, free time! Throughout my life I saw myself striving to produce little pieces of summer vacation, because that's where I thought peace would be.

But here I was, on sabbatical, with as much free time as I wanted—and I couldn't enjoy it! Even lying on the grass by the lake on a beautiful day, I didn't feel satisfied. The old antsy-ness still gnawed at me. What I was really after wasn't free time, it was peace—but the peace I craved wasn't in the free time. So where was I going to get it?

So I started talking to Jesus about my desire: "Jesus, I am spending all this energy pursuing peace and not finding it. Would you just give me some of yours?" A fundamental shift was happening inside me as I let go of what I thought would bring peace and took that desire straight to him. I was beginning to ask less and less about what I needed to do, and more and more about—well, just about *us*:

> *"Jesus, what do you like about me today?"*
> *"Tony, I like how you can plan and put things together. You are great at making complicated things easy to understand."*
>
> *"Jesus, I feel like a failure today. Who do you say that I am?"*
> *"You are mine. That's all that really matters. And I love you extravagantly."*
>
> *"Jesus, how are you proud of me?"*
> *"I'm proud of you for never giving up. Through all the pain you've had to endure, you didn't just survive: you've grown stronger. It's not hard to say, 'well done!' about that."*
> *"Just want you to know, Jesus—I'm proud of you, too."*
>
> *"Father, how am I significant to you?"*
> *I don't get words this time, but an image of being scooped up and spun around in his arms, in a loving, intimate, joyful embrace. We're dancing.*
>
> *"Jesus, I'm just wondering: are we going to sweat in heaven?"*
> *"Well," he replies, laughing, "Come and see!"*

The thing that caught my attention was that when I began to pray this way, my percentage of answered prayer suddenly jumped by about 1000%. It was as if Jesus was eagerly waiting for me ask about what he cared about most, and when I did it unleashed a flood of conversation. It wasn't that he didn't want to answer my prayers before—he just longed for us to talk about the relationship and the romance instead of just the business.

It's like in a marriage: you can get in a mode where all you talk about is paying the bills and how to discipline the kids and whose turn it is to do the dishes. It's easy to get so wrapped up in the business of life that you forget the romance of being married to a beautiful woman. You didn't get married to run a business together (I hope!)—you did it for the relationship. That's the same reason Jesus pursued you!

Talking about the Relationship

The key to talking about the relationship is to engage Jesus on the level of your desires, instead of out of your head. Desires are in all of us. We were created as human beings with a built-in yearning for things like love, acceptance, freedom, security, or belonging (see the desires diagram at right). In our original design, those needs were going to be met in our relationship with Father. Walking and talking in the garden in the cool of the day, the total acceptance, love and significance we experienced would produce an overflow to the world he gave us to invest in. Our desires were never meant to be denied or disciplined, but to be filled.

The conversation Jesus most desires with you is around filling those desires. To walk and talk with you in the cool evening: that is the desire of his heart. Deep calls to deep, and the deep desire in him is to love you well by filling the deepest part of you.

Identifying Desires

Praying your desire starts with getting in touch with the yearnings that most drive you. Is it a longing to be pursued, or to have a significant life, to come through for others, or to do well? Here's a simple process for discovering your deepest desires:

1. **Start with Strong Emotion.** *Identify a recent situation where you felt something strongly. Emotions are the easiest way to identify desires, because they bypass all the 'oughts' and 'shoulds' in our rational minds that confuse the issue.*

2. **Identify Your Response.** *What did you do in response to the situation? Did you withdraw, cry for joy, fight back, relax, try to get others to like you, or what?*

3. **Ask the Desire Question.** *Take how you responded and ask yourself, "What does that give me?" You reacted that way because you believed it would give you something—what did you think it would give you?*

4. **Drill Down.** *Ask the desire question over and over until you drill down to a desire on the chart above. (You may find this process considerably easier if you have a friend ask the questions instead of asking yourself.)*

For example, let's say you were recently in a conflict situation that stirred up strong feelings in you (step 1). The emotion you felt was fear, and your response was to withdraw and leave the room (step 2). So ask yourself, "What did it give me to leave?" (An alternate form of the desire question is, "What did I fear would happen if I *didn't* respond that way?")

The answer might be, "Withdrawing got me of the conflict." So ask again: "What did it give me to get out of the conflict?" You might say, "It preserved the relationship—I was afraid it might end." So then you would ask, "What does keeping the relationship give me?" Keep asking the desire question, and it might take you to a deep desire for belonging, to be loved or to be valued.

Finding Your Desire in Relationship

Once you've identified a desire from the desires wheel (previous page) that feels powerful for you, invite Jesus to show you how he is filling it. "Jesus, what do you see as most valuable in me?" or, "Jesus, tell me how I belong to you."

In essence, you are inviting the *relationship itself* to fill your desire for belonging or value, instead of looking to something in this world (avoiding conflict) to fill you. To give another example, in my personal story about peace I thought free time in a beautiful setting was what would give me my desire. Everything changed when I let go of the object (free time) I believed would bring peace and asked Jesus to meet my desire directly.

Unfortunately, we tend to put worldly objects like those at the center of our most passionate prayers. "Lord, please send me the man I am to marry. I know you want me to be happy." Or, "Lord, when this one deal goes through that will give me financial security, then I will give the rest of my life to missions." Or, "God release me into my ministry! I want to lead a significant life." Those prayers sound noble at first blush.

But what a terrible position to put a Father in! He longs to answer your cry, but this type of prayer asks him to *help us* attach our hearts to an object in this world, an inferior substitute for himself that is sure to wound us and leave us wanting. The choice we give him is either to help us build a house on sand, or to reap our distrust when he doesn't give us what we think we want.

The prodigal son thought getting his hands on a worldly object (his dad's money) would give him his desire: the freedom and sense of being his own man that he craved. When he received the inheritance, he used it to *remove himself from relationship* with his father by going off to a far country. But the object of his desire betrayed him, and he had to lose friendship, status, his self-respect and descend into abject poverty to discover that desire fulfilled was already waiting for him at home, in relationship with his father.

The objects we attach our desire to are like that: they cheat us out of what we most want. The person who desires acceptance puts on a mask to ensure that others will like her—and that mask prevents anyone from every getting close enough to provide the acceptance she craves. Or one who longs to live a significant life sacrifices everything in pursuit of a career, only to discover too late that he has lost his wife and children, and the best of his legacy with them.

It is not Father's will that you figure this out the hard way, like the prodigal. Simply let go and let him give you what truly satisfies your deepest longings.

James talks about the problem of attaching your desire to an object when he writes, "What causes wars, and what causes fightings among you? Is it not your passions that are at war in your members? You *desire* and do not have; so you kill. And you covet and cannot obtain; so you fight and wage war. *You do not have, because you do not ask*. You ask and do not receive, because you ask wrongly, to spend it on your passions" (James 4:1-3).

The key to understanding this passage is grasping that the subject is *desire itself*. In other words, you do not have (your desire fulfilled), because you don't ask for it. You ask (for your desire) and don't receive, because you ask for a worldly object you think will give you your desire, instead of asking Jesus to fill it directly within your relationship with him.

When you pray your desire, you aren't asking for any temporal thing. You are requesting an intimate, relational encounter with Jesus. When your Creator says you are beautiful, no one can tell you different. When the King of the Universe says you are okay, that's the final word. When the Son sets you free, you are free indeed.

Knowing His Voice

Praying your desire is not a one-way conversation. A desire prayer specifically asks for a *rhema*—a personal, experiential word from God that touches your deepest yearning. Without God speaking to you, praying your desire won't change a thing. Knowing and quoting good theology will not fill your deepest yearnings—the language of the heart isn't logic and reasoning, but living experience. Your heart longs for an intimate touch from the lover of your soul.

Hearing Jesus talk to you this way isn't hard. You just ask the question and see what wells up in your mind and heart in the next minute or two. It may be words, or an image, or just a sense of God present with you in a certain way. Then double-check if what you heard is consistent with the character of Jesus in scripture. That's all you need to do.

We make this hard because we want *proof* that what we heard is really God. We are obsessed with the question, "Is this God or just me?"—so afraid of hearing wrong that often we don't hear at all!

The question is not whether you will hear something when you pray these prayers. He will speak. The question is whether you will believe that what you hear is him.

Can it really be that simple? Well, if your question is, "Is this just me?" think about what scripture has to say about that. If this is an important question that you should be asking, one would expect that early Christians were asking it as well. And if it is as crucial a question as we make it, the New Testament would surely tell us how to differentiate between God's voice and our own ideas, wouldn't it?

If it does, I can't find any trace of it. The New Testament writers never even addressed this question in any of their letters to the churches! What does that tell you about how much effort you should be expending on this question?

I've coached hundreds of pastors, ministry leaders and everyday Christians about getting direction from God on the big decisions they face. When someone comes to me saying, "Help! I need to hear from God and I am not getting anything!" it almost always takes less than 30 minutes to discover that God *has* already been speaking and they *are* hearing—they just didn't have the confidence to believe that what they heard was really God.

So be confident—you can do this. The hardest part of praying your desire is allowing yourself to believe that the still small voice you are already hearing is the voice of God.

Desire Descriptions

Below are the 16 key desires, each with a set of related words that expand their meaning. If you aren't sure which desire you are functioning out of, use this to help you narrow it down.

Desire	Related Words
Worth	Value, validity, to be special, respect, honor
Be Known	To understand, to be understood, validity, to be seen
Joy	Happiness, delight, fun, fulfillment, satisfaction
Love	Intimacy, to be chosen, to be delighted in, interdependence, affection, relationship
Comfort	Freedom from pain, to be held, to be ministered to
Belonging	Acceptance, relationship, companionship, connection, community, family, friendship
Peace	Rest, calm, tranquility, serenity, contentment, letting go, wholeness, completion
Security	Safety, stability, order, to be protected/protect, provision, hope
To Come Through	Loyal, dependable, faithful, trustworthy
Goodness	To be right, pure, righteous, moral, character, proud of what you've done
Recognition	Affirmation, to be special, reward, honor, praise
Approval	Well done, to be acceptable, acceptance
Justice	Idealism, fairness, fighting for what's right
Freedom	Self-determination, free will, flexibility, choice, be myself, powerful, self-reliance, self-control
Significance	Legacy, achievement, changing the world, importance, influence, to be part of something larger, impact
Challenge	Purpose, meaning, a goal, risk, alive, excited, conquering something, reaching potential, winning
Physical Needs	Safety (clothing, shelter), nourishment (food, water), air, sleep, sex, exercise/activity

HOW TO USE
THIS BOOK

When was the last time you asked Jesus to tell you what he likes about you?

Questions for Jesus is an experiential guide to developing a profound intimacy with a good God, by asking him what you most long to know. If you want to go beyond rule-following, repeating the right words and asking to be bailed out, and have real conversations with Jesus, this book will help launch you on that journey.

The key to *Questions for Jesus* is that it teaches you to pray on the level of your deepest desires. For each place in Matthew's gospel where Jesus speaks to what the heart longs for, we've provided a short meditation, a set of five profound questions for Jesus, and space to record what he says when you ask.

The purpose of the meditations is for you to *experience* the story scripture is telling. The language of the heart is image, metaphor and experience, not logic or words. Therefore, connecting with Jesus at the heart level means reading these passages as stories, not as theology. You need to put yourself into them—feel them and live them. What does the setting look like? What are the characters thinking and feeling? What is at stake in the situation these people are facing? How would it impact my heart if I were there?

Each meditation is followed by five questions for Jesus that grow out of the story, provided by an author who is a world-class practitioner in the art of asking. Some questions probe what was going on inside Jesus in the situation, others ask him to directly touch a deep longing of your heart, and still others are just you and Jesus talking about your friendship. Since the best corollary on earth of the relationship between Jesus and his people is marriage, the questions are the kinds of things two people in love might ask each other.

On the journaling pages, record how each passage touches your deep desires, what Jesus says when you ask him these questions, or jot down questions of your own.

As a Devotional

There are multiple ways you can use this book. *Questions for Jesus* contains 52 meditations, so for devotional use you'd cover one passage a week for a year. We recommend you use just one of the five questions a day to get the conversation with Jesus rolling, then just respond to whatever Jesus says in whatever way seems appropriate.

This book covers only one type of prayer, so you will probably want to do other things in your devotional time as well. That's to be encouraged!

As a Journal

We've provided blank pages next to each meditation so you can write down Jesus' replies. He has a way of saying the most amazing things about you, and recording them lets you go back and drink from that revelation repeatedly.

As a Change Aid

The giants in our lives are rooted in the realm of desire. We are driven or angry or run from conflict because that response gives us something we desperately want. If you can identify the unfilled desire that drives your behavior, you can take steps to fill it within your relationship with God. And that removes the power source behind the behavior, making it much easier to change.

At the back of the book is an index showing which passages correlate with each desire. So if your change strategy includes, say, working at finding your source of approval in Jesus, you can go right to the passages on approval to pray that desire.

As a Manual on Prayer

This book is also designed to teach you the principles of how to pray intimately. For instance, the questions are carefully constructed to ask expecting a reply, from a place of faith instead of doubt, out of the assumption he is already at work instead of begging him to do something (see pages 18 and 19). Immerse yourself in the questions and you'll soon learn to construct your own.

We've also scattered short articles on desires and constructing desire prayers throughout the book to help you understand the underlying concepts.

As a Small Group Study Guide

Questions for Jesus is an exciting way to take the prayer life of your small group to a new level. Download the free *Questions for Jesus: Small Group Guide* at **www.QuestionsforJesus.net** to get started. It includes meeting outlines, discussion and debriefing questions, schedules for two 13-week classes based on the book and more. The *Guide* provides direction for daily prayer, plus group prayer exercises so you can celebrate what God is speaking to you together!

Get Training in Working with Desires

Questions for Jesus and the concept of praying your desire grew out of the Leadership MetaFormation Institute, a training organization that teaches leaders to engage life from the heart, lead others in heart transformation, and build organizational cultures where living from the heart is the normal way of life.

LMI's innovative, experiential training courses use God encounters, the arts, original music, learning games, relational teams and more to unpack how the heart works. You'll see transformational change in action, meet Jesus in your deepest desires and learn how to implement heart engaging in your world.

For more information on the Leadership MetaFormation Institute, visit our web site: **www.Meta-Formation.com** or call 800-234-2197 (U.S. Pacific Standard Time).

THE
DEVOTIONALS

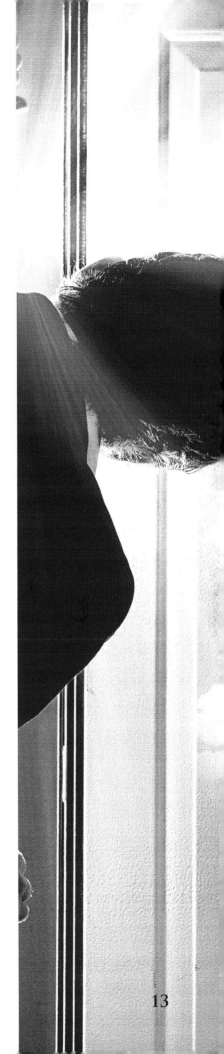

WORTH AND HONOR

Matthew 3:13-15

"Then Jesus came from Galilee to the Jordan to John, to be baptized by him. John would have prevented him, saying, 'I need to be baptized by you, and do you come to me?' But Jesus answered him, 'Let it be so now; for thus it is fitting for us to fulfill all righteousness.'"

When you stop and think about it, it is amazing that Jesus used the word 'us' to talk about himself and John in this context. John's perspective on the situation was, *You are the Messiah! I am not worthy to minister to you—it's you that should be ministering to me!* Instead, Jesus lifts him up by saying it is fitting for *us* to do this together, as a team, and that their joint act will "fulfill all righteousness."

By treating John as a peer, Jesus speaks great worth to him and his life mission. Jesus did not consider him to be a servant or a go-fer, but a friend and essential teammate.

John the Baptist's destiny was to be the forerunner of the Messiah; and he had an authority to function that went with that role. When he met Jesus, John offered to lay down that ministry and authority and give it back to Jesus, by asking Jesus to baptize him.

But instead of taking over John's role as baptizer, Jesus honors John by coming under it. He submits himself to John's call, lets John choose ('permit it at this time') how things will be done, and honors him as a partner and equal in ministry. Instead of taking over as soon as he comes on the scene, Jesus chooses to empower John to fulfill his destiny.

You are a friend, brother and co-worker of Jesus as well. He does not want to take control of you, but empower you to fulfill your destiny.

1. *Let Jesus say to you: "It is fitting for us to fulfill all righteousness." You and Jesus are co-workers in a world-changing task. Let yourself soak in that reality. Then say, "Jesus, here's how it impacts me when you say, 'us'..."*

2. *"Jesus, this passage blows up my picture of who you are—you yourself submitted to John's ministry and his authority in it. What do you want to show me about who you are through this?"*

3. *"There is a deep desire in me to be significant: to be part of something larger that makes a difference in the world. What do you appreciate about my part in your larger mission?"*

4. *"Jesus, does the thing that happened between you and John also happen between you and me—that you give me an authority for a certain mission that you yourself submit to or come under?"*

5. *"Jesus, how does it impact you to be able to do the great mission together with me?"*

JOURNAL

APPROVAL, RECOGNITION

Luke 3:22; also Matthew 3:17

"You are my beloved son, in you I am well-pleased."

At the first act of Jesus' ministry, as he formally embraces his call, Father speaks approval to his son Jesus.

When Jesus receives this great affirmation, he hasn't accomplished a thing yet in ministry. In over a decade spent toiling in obscurity, he has rarely left the backwater village he grew up in. He's run the family business—building houses and fixing tools and constructing furniture—working with his hands to support his widowed mother. That's all. Before he enters his call, before he's famous, before he teaches a word or does anything world-changing, Father's heart overflows with love, affirmation and approval for him.

The affirmation is not for what he's done, but who he is. He is a son, and that alone is greatly pleasing to God.

Interestingly, Matthew quotes what those standing nearby heard ("This is my beloved son…"); while Mark and Luke relate what the Father said directly to Jesus ("You are my beloved son…"). Jesus receives a personal word of affirmation from the Father, and at the same time is affirmed publicly in who he is. Father wants everyone to know how pleased he is with his son.

To understand the impact of this passage, remember that at this point in Jesus' life, only two people in the whole world know who he really is—his mother and John—and one of them he has just met. For 30 years, Jesus was unrecognized and unseen, constantly underestimated, told he was less than who he was, knowing that no one really knew him. To hear "You are my beloved son" spoke identity, worth and belonging to Jesus.

On this day, Jesus puts on his destiny for the first time, and is finally known for who he really is: by his Father, by the prophet and by the crowd.

1. *Let Jesus say to you: "You are my beloved son, in whom I am well pleased." Soak in it. Let those words sink into your heart.*

2. *"Jesus, how am I a son to you? What do you love about me as a son?"*

3. *"Jesus, what was it like for you to have no one know who you were for so long? How did you deal with that?"*

4. *"Who do you see me as that nobody else knows?"*

5. *"How have I operated like a son this week? What does that do for you when I operate that way?"*

JOURNAL

CONSTRUCT YOUR OWN
DESIRE PRAYERS

The prayers in this book are based on a set of simple principles about praying your desire. Each principle is listed below with examples to clarify the meaning.

Touch Deep Desires

A desire prayer is a request for a specific member of the trinity to touch a specific deep desire from the desires wheel (see page 7). We may ask how he sees us ("Jesus, how am I beautiful to you today?"), what he believes about us ("Okay, why do *you* think I can do this?"), why he treats us so well, what he has done for us that we don't realize ("How have you been pursuing me for the last 24 hours?") or what he feels ("How did it impact you when I prayed for that lady and she got set free?") Desire prayers require you to dig deep and ask about what you really care about.

Believe in God's Goodness

Desire prayers are rooted in addressing a good God who is totally for you. The wording of the prayer assumes that God is already acting on your behalf, instead of pleading as if he had to be begged to act. So instead of praying, "Father, *do* you love me?" ask, "Father, *how* do you love me? Or rather than saying, "Jesus would you give me your peace?" pray, "Jesus, *how have you been* giving your peace to me today?" Pray from faith that he is already operating out of love toward you instead of praying in a way that expresses doubt about his good intentions.

Are About the Relationship, Not the Business

My wife and I run a business together, and unless we are careful we can end up talking about cash flows and action steps and employee problems—and never experience the romance of being married. Desire prayers are about the romantic side of your relationship with God. Instead of asking about the business ("What should I *do* today?") you ask about the relationship ("What do you *love* about me today?") Desire prayers are about love, acceptance, security, significance, freedom— the desires that are touched by relational intimacy—and not about making changes, repenting for mistakes or getting things done.

Receive Instead of Strive

It's Father's delight to fill our desires with himself, to give and see us receive. However, we're often so used to praying in a 'doing' mode that we don't enter a receiving posture where he can fill us. A desire prayer is about how Jesus is touching your heart, not about what you ought to do to make that happen. For instance, instead of praying, "Jesus, help *me* to live out of peace," ask, "Jesus, how have *you* been bringing peace to me today?" Or instead of "Father, how can *I* put on love today?" ask, "Father, how do *you* love me today?"

Ask for an Experiential Word (*Rhema*)

A funny thing often happens when we first try to pray our desire. Instead of waiting for Jesus to answer the question, we begin to recite the religious principles we've been taught in the past. In other words, we instinctively substitute head knowledge for heart encounter. Desire prayers are a request for a rhema: that Jesus would speak a personal, immediate, living word to us in the moment. Praying your desire is about having a dynamic conversation, not reciting theology. This is a place where the written word (logos) cannot take the place of the conversational word (rhema), because hearing the experiential rhema creates faith in ways that the written word can't (see Romans 10:17).

Are Tested by the Word (*Logos*)

When you hear something, check it against what you know of scripture and the character of Jesus. The sheep know his voice—so ask, "Does this sound like him?" If you pray, "What do you like about me today?" and hear, "Nothing—you are a total failure," that's not consistent with scripture and it doesn't sound like someone who went out of his way to die for us! Steeping yourself in the Bible is a vital part of praying your desire. Without the *logos* to check our *rhema* experiences against, we'd probably start to get weird pretty quickly.

SIGNIFICANCE

Matthew 4:18-20

"As he walked by the Sea of Galilee, he saw two brothers, Simon who is called Peter and Andrew his brother, casting a net into the sea; for they were fishermen. And he said to them, 'Follow me, and I will make you fishers of men.' Immediately they left their nets and followed him."

Jesus calls all of us to be part of a great adventure with him. But here, the invitation comes to men trapped in the daily grind of making a living and raising a family. Laboring in the dangerous, grueling occupation of fishing, they worked long days (or nights), missing out on much of the social life of the community. These businessmen owned their own boats, sold their own product and

often traveled to market it. They spoke multiple languages and saw more of the world than most.

However, their opportunities were constricted in ways we can hardly fathom. They would be fishermen like their fathers, for all their lives, working in one small town. Their schedule would be dictated by the weather and the seasons, their behavior guided by the strict expectations of their community and their religion.

Then Jesus passes by, detonating their world with a call to the kind of significant life they had barely thought possible. That they left everything right there on the beach and never came back speaks something of their state of mind. Were they dissatisfied with their lot in life? Hungry for something more? Desperate for anything that might break the monotony?

But now, instead of catching fish, they would catch people. Instead of fighting the waves to put food on the table, they would campaign for an eternal purpose. Men with no opportunity for advancement had suddenly been given a chance for more. Jesus was calling a high D on the DISC (Peter) to do something worthy of his energy and abilities—touching the D's desire for challenge and significance—and Peter jumped at the chance.

1. *"Jesus, what did you experience when you called to Peter and Andrew on the beach and they jumped up, left their work and ran after you? How did that touch your heart?"*

2. *"What is one place in my life where you see more in me than I do in myself?"*

3. *"These guys became some of your closest friends. What did you see in them that caused you to invite them into your inner circle? What do you see in me that led you to give me that same invitation?"*

4. *"You called these guys in a way that validated their life experience—what they knew was fishing, and you called them to be fishers of men. Everything they'd ever learned you put to use. What in my past have I discarded as unspiritual or commonplace that you are actually building my destiny on?"*

5. *"What did those guys mean to you during your life here on earth?"*

JOURNAL

JUSTICE

Matthew 5:1-3

"When Jesus saw his ministry drawing huge crowds, he climbed a hillside. Those who were apprenticed to him, the committed, climbed with him. Arriving at a quiet place, he sat down and taught his climbing companions. This is what he said: 'You're blessed when you're at the end of your rope. With less of you there is more of God and his rule.'" (MSG)

"When Jesus saw the crowds, He went up on the mountain; and after He sat down, His disciples came to Him. He opened His mouth and began to teach them, saying, 'Blessed are the poor in spirit, for theirs is the kingdom of heaven.'"

Jesus touched a whole range of desires in the Sermon on the Mount, a message meant to 'draw all men unto him' by speaking to the deep longings of their hearts. Whether it's justice for the poor, an incredible inheritance for those who don't grasp after things, or comfort for the hurting, every deep desire is filled in the Kingdom of Heaven. The beatitudes are where Jesus lays out his notion of desire fulfilled as a tree of life.

He speaks to a nation under the boot of a foreign conqueror and subject to crippling taxes. The tax system was designed to attract the most ruthless and unethical operators—the sole income of these private sub-contractors was how much money above the actual tax rate they could extort from their countrymen. There were taxes on land and income, poll taxes, sales taxes, bridge and road tolls, town dues, temple taxes, import/export duties…

When we experience injustice, it is easy to get caught up in anger and frustration at our circumstances. Yet Jesus says that desire fulfilled comes from focusing on the justice of heaven, not the injustice on earth. To get angry about your taxes or complain about how the system takes advantage of you goes nowhere.

Jesus' invitation to life is, "Think this way: you are actually fortunate if you experience poverty or injustice now! The sooner you realize your desires can never be filled in this world, the more attached your heart will become to heaven."

The poor in this life have whole kingdoms coming to them, and will live like kings in heaven. There is justice in the Kingdom of God, and you will experience it, and it will fill your desire for all things to be well. Loss or deprivation in this life only destines you for fullness in this better Kingdom.

1. *"What is something in life that I've seen as loss that actually made room in me for more of you?"*

2. *"Jesus, what goes on in your heart when you look at the poor? Let me experience some of what you experience when you look at them."*

3. *"Jesus, here is my anger at the injustice I've experienced. What do you want to give me in return?"*

4. *"Jesus, I experienced a big loss when _____. How will you fill that desire in Heaven?"*

5. *"Jesus, what can I let go of today to experience desire fulfilled in the Kingdom of Heaven?"*

JOURNAL

COMFORT

Matthew 5:4

"You're blessed when you feel you've lost what is most dear to you. Only then can you be embraced by the One most dear to you." (MSG)

"Blessed are those who mourn, for they shall be comforted."

Here Jesus speaks to the deep desire for peace (comfort, freedom from pain) of those who mourn the hurts and losses of the world. Interestingly, the Greek word for "comfort" has a second meaning: to urge, encourage, implore or plead. Holy Spirit who comforts us is at the same time imploring and urging Father to take action on our behalf. The Comforter is simultaneously the Intercessor; and the comfort of the Holy Spirit is joined at the hip to the Godhead fighting on our behalf.

To be in Spirit's presence is to be comforted, because that's who he is. Every whisper of his voice is both a comfort and an urging to jump in, to come deeper, to embrace the Kingdom of Heaven. Spirit's call to holiness is wrapped in comfort, in exactly the same way that his comfort is wrapped in intercession. The way we know the Comforter's voice is that he always enters us as peace and calls us to glory.

And Holy Spirit is eternally, relentlessly for us, always encouraging Father to show himself on our behalf. You cannot intercede without being for the person on whose behalf you are praying. In the same way, the Intercessor is always on our side. The way we know the Intercessor's voice is that he always believes and wants the best for us.

1. *"Comforter, here's what I am mourning: _____. Let me experience who you are in this."*

2. *"Comforter, show me your Intercessor side. When you are comforting my mourning, what are you imploring Father to do at the same time?"*

3. *"Comforter, what does comfort mean to you? And what does peace mean?"*

4. *"Father, you experience loss every day when we do stupid things, and you grieve over it like Jesus wept over Jerusalem. And yet the Spirit that is you is called the 'Comforter.' How does comfort come in the midst of that? How do you grieve and still remain God?"*

5. *"Father, you chose to lose what was most dear—your Son. And Jesus, you lost what was most dear to you as well: your relationship with Father was severed on the cross. Help me understand what that choice meant to you."*

JOURNAL

....
....
....
....
....
....
....
....
....
....
....
....
....
....
....
....
....
....
....
....
....
....
....
....
....

CONTENTMENT

Matthew 5:5

"You're blessed when you're content with just who you are—no more, no less. That's the moment you find yourselves proud owners of everything that can't be bought." (MSG)

"Blessed are the gentle, for they shall inherit the earth."

Think for a minute about what it would mean to inherit the earth. Is there a special place you've always wanted to live? It's yours! Want to pad out in your bathrobe to enjoy a cup of freshly-ground coffee and a spectacular sunrise off your veranda? Done! Do you dream of traveling to Bora Bora to paddle all day in the teal waters over the coral reef? Your private jet is waiting at the airport. Anything else you need? Because the resources of an entire planet are on call.

Jesus speaks of an extravagant reward for those who don't put themselves forward or try to take what they think they deserve. 'Let go, and it will all come to you as a special gift from me,' is the message. Those willing to let go of meeting their desires in things, will experience their

desire fulfilled—and get things in spades in the Kingdom of Heaven to boot.

The gentle will inherit the earth for a simple reason: because everyone else will want them to! The gentle treat other people right, and so others are drawn to them, trust them, and return the honor they are given. The gentle are creators of friendship, fairness and fulfilled desire in relationship. The gentle don't hang on to things, but distribute them to touch the desires of others

This principle plays out relationally on earth, but in heaven it becomes a physical reality. The gentle walk in an authority here in the realm of the heart, because they know how to honor the heart. And in heaven, the realm where the inward heart and spirit come to the fore, so does the authority of the gentle. The whole crowd of heaven will delight to say of the gentle, 'They did so well at holding things lightly on earth that we were all blessed—so let's give them the whole planet!

1. *"Jesus, what does it give you to take the ones who got the least in this life and give them the best in heaven? What makes you take so much joy in turning the world on its head?"*

2. *"Jesus, how were you meek (not grasping or putting yourself forward) in life? I'd like to get to know that side of you better."*

3. *"Where do you see gentleness in me? What do you love about that?"*

4. *"How have you been gentle toward me this week?"*

5. *"Who around me looks like you in this area? Who carries your gentleness well? What can I learn about who you are from watching them?"*

JOURNAL

OBSTACLES

A while back I coached a very intelligent leader who was struggling in her relationship with God. "I try to ask these desire questions and just don't hear anything!" she declaimed wearily. "It's like God just ignores me or he's forgotten about me or something."

I could identify—I've felt like giving up on hearing God's voice at times, too. But wanting to know more, I said, "Well, let's try a desire prayer and see what happens. Take 30 seconds and ask Jesus something, like, 'What do you love about me today?'"

Half a minute later she responded. "Okay, here's what I got—but this is probably just in my head. You know, something I thought of in the moment. I don't want to misrepresent God or anything."

"So what did you get?"

"Well, like I said, this is probably just me. I was thinking he loves how I stick to things and don't give up."

"Is that what God said?"

"Um… I guess it could be."

"Can you make a decision here? Is that God or isn't it?"

"I'm not sure."

"Alright, let's try again. Hearing God is a process, not a test. You learn how to do it bit by bit. How about this question: 'Jesus, how am I like you?'"

I waited a bit, then she spoke up, disappointment obvious in her voice. "I didn't really hear anything."

"Say more about that."

"My mind was wandering and stuff. It doesn't seem like anything was from God, though: just my own thoughts."

"Which were…?"

"Okay, here's what popped into my head. I was thinking about my grandson, and then I thought that one way I might be like him is that I set boundaries as a parent. I think ahead about what might go wrong or how Johnny might get hurt, and I try to help him stay out of those situations. But that seems like just my own thoughts. Just because it popped into my head doesn't mean it was God."

"That sounds like something he would say."

"Well… maybe. It's possible."

"You're equivocating. Can you take the 'maybe' out of that sentence?"

"I guess. That could be God's voice."

I chuckled to myself at her unsuccessful attempt to stop equivocating, then offered, "Okay, try one more. 'Jesus, how have you been active in my life in the last 24 hours?'"

After a quiet moment she replied. "My grandson is with us today, so I was thinking how that makes me slow down and be more in the moment. That's something I've been praying to get better at. But—it was just a thought," she added hurriedly. "It's not—I'm not sure I was really hearing God there."

"So if you were really hearing God, what would it sound like?"

"I guess… that I would *know* it's him. Every so often God hits me over the head with a baseball bat, and confirms it in different ways, and I just know it's him. I guess I'm just a person who needs a two-by-four approach."

"So what I'm hearing is, you want God to hit you over the head with that two-by-four on a daily basis, so you know for sure he is speaking?"

"Well, not when you put it like that."

"So what *do* you want?"

"I guess I just want to hear his still small voice, that's all. I want to learn to hear him speak gently and not always with the baseball bat. Is that too much to ask?"

"No, that's a great thing to ask for," I replied.

"So, let me make an observation. How many times did you say 'maybe' or 'probably' or 'I guess' or 'I think' or 'I could' in the last ten minutes?"

She laughed nervously. "A lot—*probably.*"

At that we both laughed.

"Did you notice how much energy you spent trying to convince me—and yourself!—that Jesus wasn't speaking to you? Each time we prayed something came to you, but it was very difficult for you to say anything was from God without adding a 'probably' or 'maybe' to it. It seems like you are protecting your heart: that if you really let yourself believe that this was him, something bad would happen to you. Does that make sense?"

"Yeah, it does. I guess I'm afraid of being disappointed again. I've felt ignored and not seen so many times that opening the door to let myself believe is probably just too painful. Look—I did it again! I just said 'probably.'"

"Good insight. So every time Jesus tries to speak gently, that reaction is the barrier he has to break through. All that energy being expended to prove that it isn't him, to explain it away. All the memories and the fear of being disappointed. That's a huge wall to climb."

"Wow. I never realized that before."

"Can you see now why you believe God has to hit you with a two-by-four?"

"Yeah—whenever he speaks gently I block it out."

"Would you like to change that?"

"Yes! But… but I don't know how."

"Tell you what—here's an experiment you can try. You decide if this sounds compelling, and don't do it unless you really want to. How about if for one week you decided to believe that what you heard was God? You didn't question it, try to explain it away or say it was all in your head, but just accepted that God was speaking. What do you think of that idea?"

"Wow. That sounds risky. Kind of exhilarating though, too."

"What's the risk?"

"That I'll be disappointed—that God will ignore me, and I won't hear anything again."

"And if you keep doing what you are doing now—if you keep that wall up—will you hear anything?"

"No. That sort of guarantees I won't hear, doesn't it? The wall I was using to protect myself from being disappointed is actually keeping me from the thing I want most—intimacy with God. So staying put gives me nothing."

"So what do you think?"

"Alright—I'll give it a try!"

GOODNESS

Matthew 5:6

"You're blessed when you've worked up a good appetite for God. He's food and drink in the best meal you'll ever eat." (MSG)

"Blessed are those who hunger and thirst for righteousness, for they shall be satisfied."

Often our hunger and thirst for goodness takes shape in a battle of competing voices. Our faith tells us about a Son of God who loved us enough to die for us, while our overactive inner critic says we are undeserving screw-ups. We long for the solid experience of knowing that we are okay, that we've done well with our lives.

Jesus speaks to this yearning for goodness with a simple food analogy. If you hunger for righteousness, you will get a ticket to the all-you-can-eat buffet. If your throat is parched in a thirst to be okay with God, you will have an eternity of free refills. The price of entry to the banquet is not what the Jewish culture assumed—doing good things—but simply to be hungry. Desire fulfilled is there for the asking.

The word translated "satisfied"(chortazo) is used in the New Testament when people are full after eating, like at the feeding of the 4000, where "they all ate and were satisfied (chortazo) (Luke 9:17)." It's also used by Paul in Philippians 4:12: "I have learned the secret of being filled (chortazo) and going hungry, both of having abundance and suffering need: I can do all things through him who strengthens me." When Jesus touches your desire, it is as filling as a good meal.

Words of life from Jesus are a powerful antidote to an overwrought conscience that says we aren't welcome at the banquet. Therefore, "since we have confidence to enter the holy place by the blood of Jesus… let us draw near with a sincere heart in full assurance of faith, having our hearts sprinkled clean from an evil conscience…" (Hebrew 10:19-22).

1. *"Jesus, what's on today's menu? How do you want to satisfy my desire for goodness today?"*

2. *"Jesus, what would you say today to my inner critic—the voice that is always telling me I am not good enough for you?"*

3. *"Jesus, how have I treated you well lately? How have I been good to you?"*

4. *"Thanks for believing in my desire to be good and do well, Jesus. And thanks for dealing with me according to my best desires and not my worst."*

5. *"Jesus, what will it be like to have my desire for goodness fully satisfied in heaven? Can you lift the veil a bit and show me?"*

JOURNAL

···

···

···

···

···

···

···

···

···

···

···

···

···

···

···

···

···

···

···

···

···

···

···

···

···

···

SECURITY, BEING KNOWN

Matthew 5:7

"You're blessed when you care. At the moment of being 'care-full,' you find yourselves cared for." (MSG)

"Blessed are the merciful, for they shall receive mercy."

Mercy is compassionate treatment or forbearance, especially in situations where it is undeserved. To be merciful is to forgive offenders and run to comfort those who are in pain and alleviate their distress.

Mercy appears as a gift in Romans 12, a list that describes different personality types. Those with this gift of mercy are tender-hearted, easily touched by the needs and wounds of others. They're the ones who root for the underdog, take in strays, are on the look-out for the marginalized and make the outsiders feel welcome.

Jesus addresses those he created for emotional sensitivity, who by this design are also the most easily wounded, and promises the comfort and security they long for. "You who open your hearts

to others, who are willing to enter into their pain, will find that my heart is always open to you, and I will be your healer." The compassion-givers will receive a compassion that fills their desire to overflowing. He sees and knows what you have given. Jesus is satisfied by your gift; and he will cross the universe to satisfy your longing for mercy.

But make no mistake: this is not a weak, cowering mercy, powerless to resist the cruel blows the world dishes out. The gentle compassion of Jesus is wrapped in the furious will of a she-bear protecting her cubs. It is a force of nature, a crushing tsunami rushing down from heaven to protect and defend his own, wielding the power to upend circumstances and change nations on your behalf. His irresistible tenderness looks on our weakness and misery and says, "I *will* make this glorious! I *will* bind up your wounds and redeem this pain, and no power in heaven or earth can stop me."

Father's mercy and Jesus' compassion are there for the asking. Let's ask!

1. *"Jesus, I long to live in a place where a gentle word is rewarded with gentleness, and an act of compassion with compassion—where human cruelty isn't part of the equation. Tell me about what that will be like in heaven."*

2. *"Here's where I hurt and long for mercy: _____. How do you want to touch that today?"*

3. *"Jesus, you've experienced this verse. You know what it is like to live with an open your heart in a cruel world, and then you tasted the mercy of heaven. What was it like for you to go from torture here to glory there?"*

4. *"Jesus, tell me about your desire to reach down and show mercy to me. I want to understand why you do what you do."*

5. *"How has your mercy been following me in the last week?"*

JOURNAL

GOODNESS

Matthew 5:8

"Blessed are the pure in heart, for they shall see God."

"You're blessed when you get your inside world—your mind and heart—put right. Then you can see God in the outside world." (MSG)

I vividly remember two particular customers from my days as a furniture designer. One embodied purity in heart. She had come from a non-Christian family, and just decided one day as a little girl that she needed to go to church. So every Sunday she dressed up and walked to church all by herself!

Her defining quality was her grateful attitude and sunny disposition. We built her a custom-designed, hand-made cherry bed with her family crest carved into the headboard. She thoroughly enjoyed every step of the process. She would come in and watch as the piece came together, compliment the craftsmen, ooh and aah over it. And everything—*everything*—in the process of building that piece went well. No problems, no mistakes. That amazing bed ended up being published in a book.

A year later, I developed a beautiful design for a set of bookcases for another customer. She was demanding, meticulous and suspicious of being taken advantage of. On that project, we couldn't seem to do anything right. The carvings were disappointingly executed. We kept having delays. The finish involved bleaching the wood, and it came out horrible—we had to strip the whole thing down and do it all over again. It was as if her attitude poisoned the whole project.

I saw the same principle at work with many other clients over the years. The pure in heart—the ones with clean consciences and a grateful attitude, who weren't operating out of woundedness—saw beauty and honest effort and integrity in the process. Their projects always seemed to go especially well. With the wounded, suspicious and negative clients, problems cropped up at every turn. No matter how hard we tried, they were rarely satisfied.

When your inside world is wounded and dirty, you see life through that lens, and everywhere you look is dishonesty and corruption. When your inside world is pure, you see God in the outside world.

Hearts that are healed and clean see God at work in all things. The pure in heart gain what they have longed for and devoted their lives to—to see and understand and experience God. It is really true—happy and fortunate are those with a pure heart!

1. *"What do you see as pure in heart about me?"*

2. *"Jesus, what was it like to look out on the world from a totally pure heart? How did that make your perspective different than mine?"*

3. *"Father, show me life through your pure eyes. Where are you present in my world today?"*

4. *"Jesus, I long to be whole and pure. How have you been responding to that yearning in me?"*

5. *"Father, I just wanted you to know I am really anticipating seeing you and Jesus in heaven. Let me tell you what that will mean to me…"*

JOURNAL

PEACE

Matthew 5:9

"Blessed are the peacemakers, for they will be called Sons of God." (NIV)

"You're blessed when you can show people how to cooperate instead of compete or fight. That's when you discover who you really are, and your place in God's family." (MSG)

There gathered on a gentle slope, overlooking the seascape of Galilee, Jesus spoke to the gathering crowd. Whenever a crowd gathers, there is a mixed bag of motives, thoughts and feelings, desires and dreams. Peace is often not evident. Imagine yourself among that throng, coming to meet the prophet who healed a friend of yours, who called together a group of unlikely men (tax collectors, fishermen and sinners) and revolutionized their lives, whose words were strangely drawing yet unsettling. You bring your own desire to be healed, to do significant works or to find a transforming truth to live by—your own need and yearning, mixed and churning.

As the crowd settles and Jesus begins to speak, his presence says more than his words. Something in his spirit *is* peace, pulling open the hunger in your heart. Instead of giving you rules to follow, he gazes into your eyes and paints a picture of what it is like to live out of the identity of the true Kingdom. His word painting calls you out of the everyday into a place of greatness. Your heart leaps, seeing yourself as one who brings peace to others, and you begin to experience what it might be like to walk in the world as a child of God.

And this is the calling: not to *strive* towards quieting our own churning hearts, or to face into the fray of human conflict fearlessly, but to seek to live in the presence of the Prince of Peace. We are called to know our true identity as sons and daughters, and to learn to be part of a family living out the family ethos.

The place of peace is always in belonging, for it is in belonging that we find out who we truly are. As children of the Most High, we are made in his image, and our deepest desires are met as we learn to live from a place of uncontested identity.

You are already blessed, happy, deeply fulfilled for you *are* a child of God, and as such, a carrier of peace in the world.

1. *"Jesus, how do I already carry your peace?"*

2. *"Daddy, what are the ways that I look just like you?"*

3. *"Spirit, if your peace was all over me today, what would that look like?"*

4. *"Jesus, tell me again what it is like to be a Son of God and to walk in the greatness you have called me to."*

5. *"Papa, what quality do you see in me that most reminds you of my brother, Jesus?"*

JOURNAL

BELONGING, BEING UNDERSTOOD

Matthew 5:10-12

"You're blessed when your commitment to God provokes persecution. The persecution drives you even deeper into God's kingdom. Not only that—count yourselves blessed every time people put you down or throw you out or speak lies about you to discredit me. What it means is that the truth is too close for comfort and they are uncomfortable. You can be glad when that happens—give a cheer, even!—for though they don't like it, I do! And all heaven applauds. And know that you are in good company. My prophets and witnesses have always gotten into this kind of trouble." (MSG)

Have you ever lived in a different country or culture? Or married into a family that is very different than your own: on the opposite side of the political, educational or socio-economic spectrum?

Or imagine attending a church that is very, very unlike your own. If you are Baptist, envision joining a Congregational church. If you are Quaker, go fundamentalist. Or if you are charismatic, assume the only church for 50 miles around is Cessationist.

When you are in a group that thinks completely different than you do, being understood becomes a powerful desire. Matthew was writing to Jewish believers in a time of tension between followers of Jesus and traditional Jews. His readers saw themselves as a part of the synagogue, and saw their faith as a fulfillment of Judaism. Yet that was a stance which many Jews refused to accept. Finally, around 85 A.D., a phrase was inserted into the synagogue liturgy pronouncing a curse on "Nazarenes and heretics" which made the split irrevocable. The Jewish Christians had been disowned by their ancestral faith and their country.

Where in your life are you around people who don't think like you do, or don't agree with your faith? In the moments when people rag on you for your beliefs, make fun of your positions or imply you are stupid for thinking what you do, Jesus calls you blessed, favored, even happy! The fact that you don't fit in this world marks you as belonging to the Kingdom of Heaven. In fact, you are in great company—Jesus knows exactly how you feel.

You who don't fit in the world belong to a community in heaven that knows you, deeply honors your faith and celebrates who you are. You are understood by a dear friend who holds your heart gently—so gently that he can handle a bruised blade of grass without breaking it. And you are cheered on by a great cloud of witnesses who are on your side.

Allow yourself to soak in that truth—that to be misunderstood and mistreated by the world is the shared mark of the company of heaven.

1. *"Jesus, I felt misunderstood and judged when _____. When have you felt like that?"*

2. *"What does it mean to you that I belong to the house of heaven?"*

3. *"Tell me more about relationships in heaven. What will it be like to belong there?"*

4. *"Jesus, what do you want to say to me in those moments when I feel like I don't belong?"*

5. *"In some ways, my faith has been rejected by my country. Who do you want to be to me there?"*

JOURNAL

VALIDATION, WORTH

Matthew 5:13-16

"You are the salt of the earth; but if salt has lost its taste, how shall its saltness be restored? It is no longer good for anything except to be thrown out and trodden under foot by men. You are the light of the world. A city set on a hill cannot be hid. Nor do men light a lamp and put it under a bushel, but on a stand, and it gives light to all in the house. Let your light so shine before men, that they may see your good works and give glory to your Father who is in heaven."

Here, Jesus tells his Jewish hearers who they really are. He is reinstating their identity as influencers and messengers of the one God to the rest of the world. "You are the salt of the earth," and "you are the light of the world" refer to their calling as God's chosen people.

That's what your true identity is as well. You display the greatness of the image of God, and Jesus calls you to let the world see it. Who you are is good, and God knows and approves of that identity. And this glory in you is completely obvious—like a brightly-lit city shining in the night, high on a hill.

I once visited ancient Pergamum in Turkey. Perched on a steep, solitary pinnacle a thousand

feet high, the city dominated the plain for miles around. When you drive up the valley, your eye is immediately captured by a gleaming white-marble temple shining from the apex of the hill like a beacon. You literally can't miss it. In fact, it was designed to be seen—to sway those who saw it with awe of the city's wealth, power and importance.

When Jesus' hearers pictured a city on a hill, they thought of Jerusalem. The radiant temple with its marble, bronze and gold would have stood high above every other structure, on a giant platform of beautifully-quarried stones. All roads led to it, and any pilgrim approaching the city could have seen it while still far away. It was the symbol of their nation and the center of their universe.

And that is the image Jesus chose to describe the glory you carry.

1. *"Jesus, what is my glory?"*

2. *"What's one way that I am created in your image that I haven't realized yet?"*

3. *"You used a city on a hill and putting a light under a basket as analogies for not hiding who I am in you. What kind of analogies would you use today?"*

4. *"How am I salty? How do I spice up the world?"*

5. *"Jesus, what about my life brings glory to Father?"*

JOURNAL

....
....
....
....
....
....
....
....
....
....
....
....
....
....
....
....
....
....
....
....
....
....
....
....

PHYSICAL NEEDS

Matthew 6:11

"Give us this day our daily bread…"

It's okay to ask Papa God to meet your basic physical needs. And not merely okay—it is his delight to enter into the simple things of daily life with you. The everyday routines, from the chores to the snores, are all part of your shared life. He loves changing a diaper with you as much as doing ministry together.

In the physical as well as the psychological realms, Father is the filler of needs and desires. Like a father seeing the perfect gift for his daughter and buying it on impulse, he is thinking of how to love you well at each moment. And like parents working a job and handling the finances to provide for a toddler who is blissfully unaware of money, he acts behind the scenes in ways we don't see or understand to take care of us.

Just as it is good to come directly to him to fill our desires, it is good to depend on him for our daily bread. "Give us this day…" is not meant to be a plea couched in doubt and desperation, but a grateful, happy dependence: "Just like you have every other day, give us *this* day as well our daily bread. You have been so faithful, I have come to trust you each day, and I am willing to trust you for the next one, too."

That security goes beyond job security and social security, beyond knowing you have a paycheck coming or that you have money in the bank. It's big enough to release your children's future to, big enough to entrust your spouse (or if you will ever have a spouse) to, full enough to let go of your destiny and not lack. It's big enough for good times and bad, when everything is coming up roses and while everything is falling apart. In every detail of life, the big guy is looking out for you.

1. *"Father, how does it touch you as a father when I trust you to meet my basic needs?"*

2. *"How have you planned to let me experience you as provider today?"*

3. *"Daddy, I'd sleep better knowing you'll take care of _____. Tell me one more time why I can trust you there."*

4. *"Father, tell me about how I'm more secure in you than I am in my job, my skills or my savings."*

5. *"Father, what gift do you want to give me today?"*

JOURNAL

SECURITY, BEING KNOWN

Matthew 6:25-34

"Therefore I tell you, do not be anxious about your life, what you shall eat or what you shall drink, nor about your body, what you shall put on. Is not life more than food, and the body more than clothing? Look at the birds of the air: they neither sow nor reap nor gather into barns, and yet your heavenly Father feeds them. Are you not of more value than they? And which of you by being anxious can add one cubit to his span of life? And why are you anxious about clothing? Consider the lilies of the field, how they grow; they neither toil nor spin; yet I tell you, even Solomon in all his glory was not arrayed like one of these. But if God so clothes the grass of the field, which today is alive and tomorrow is thrown into the oven, will he not much more clothe you, O men of little faith? Therefore do not be anxious, saying, 'What shall we eat?' or 'What shall we drink?' or 'What shall we wear?' For the Gentiles seek all these things; and your heavenly Father knows that you need them all. But seek first his kingdom and his righteousness, and all these things shall be yours as well."

In this passage, Jesus is speaking to the desire for security—to know that our basic needs will be met, that we will be provided for. Instead of focusing on our needs or casting round to see where we could find food or shelter, Jesus asks us to tune into a revelation we can see all around us: how God provides for all of creation. The birds are fed each day even though they don't plan ahead, and the flowers look gorgeous without their even trying. See how God takes care of even the smallest details like these? His care for someone he loves as much as you is much more extravagant.

Jesus is also speaking to the twisted desire of anxiety—of trying to foresee pain, of attempting to control what goes on in our lives and be hyper-alert so we won't get hurt again. Anxiety is often accompanied by a protective belief: that if I anxiously plan and try to control what happens to me, my life will be longer and better. Laughing, Jesus asks, "Does your worried planning add even a day to your span of life? Do your protective strategies really make your life more full—or do they cut you off from life and keep you empty?"

He smiles. "Now, when you actually put that belief in words and say it out loud, it sounds kind of silly, doesn't it? You are already fully known by Father, and he sees exactly what you need. Let go of trying to control what you have no power over! You are worth so much to Father and I, and we are always watching out for you."

1. *You are of much more value than the birds Father feeds and the flowers he beautifully clothes. Soak in that revelation—let yourself rest in it.*

2. *"Father, how have you been watching out for me in the last 24 hours?"*

3. *"Father, I have a deep desire to be secure and protected. Show me how I have that in you."*

4. *"Daddy, I'm anxious about: _____. Make me laugh—why does that look silly to you?"*

5. *"What do you want to clothe me in today?"*

JOURNAL

LOVE, TO COME THROUGH

Matthew 7:7-11

"Just ask and it will be given to you; seek after it and you will find. Continue to knock and the door will be opened for you. All who ask receive. Those who seek, find what they seek. And he who knocks, will have the door opened. Think of it this way: if your son asked you for bread, would you give him a stone? Of course not—you would give him a loaf of bread. If your son asked for a fish, would you give him a snake? No, to be sure, you would give him a fish—the best fish you could find. So if you, who are sinful, know how to give your children good gifts, how much more so does your Father in heaven, who is perfect, know how to give great gifts to His children!" (Voice)

Just ask. It will be given. Knock. It will be opened. Seek. It will be found.

Such straightforward promises, with no twist, no maze of right moves we need to make in order to find the prize! There is no treasure map to lead us to a buried, rusty key that only the elite can discover and enter some special chamber.

The disciples, reared in a world of rules, have incredulous looks on their faces as they listen to these words. Isn't there something we have to figure out, some special wisdom or talent that will make us worthy of receiving what we most desire? Can it be that the ways of the kingdom are so easily unveiled?

If not, then why do prayers often seem so empty?

Looking into their eyes, Jesus sees the longing, and also the unanswered questions. So he goes on to explain: "It's all about being Papa's child. It's about knowing the goodness of the heart of the Father for you, and asking from a place of childlike trust."

Jesus paints the picture of a dad who gives a child a stone for supper; or hands him a snake when he's hungry for a fish taco. Would you do this to your son? Of course not! In this picture of a parent they understand: Abba loves me. He loves to be good to me because I *belong* to him. He needs no other reason. Father loves to hear my desires and meet them.

So just ask. Just seek. Just knock. You are the adored child who belongs to the Father. He has good gifts and has your best in mind.

1. *"Daddy, what do you want to give me today? I know you give good gifts and I'm ready to receive!"*

2. *"Papa, it's me—your favorite child. What are you celebrating about me today?"*

3. *"Jesus, what is something you love about our Dad that you want to remind me of today?"*

4. *"Papa, how do you feel when I come knocking at your door?"*

5. Coming up a walkway, you approach a rustic wooden door. Laughter and voices of delight filter through from the other side. At your timid knock, the door flies open, and Papa, Brother and Sister shout with glee at your arrival, and run to fetch the gifts they've prepared… Ask, *"What gift do you have ready for me today?"*

JOURNAL

TYPES OF
DESIRE PRAYERS

It's a great adventure to create your own desire prayers! Here are some different forms to try:

1. Ask Jesus how he sees you or feels about you.
    "Jesus, what do you love about me today?"

2. Ask Jesus to tell you who you are.
    "When I can't finish a project, I feel like I am a failure. Who am I in your eyes?"

3. Ask him to touch a deep desire in you.
    "Jesus, I have a deep desire for peace right now. How do you want to touch me there?"

4. Ask what he has been doing for you lately that you don't see.
    "Jesus, how have you been pursuing me this week?"

5. Ask how something impacts Jesus' heart.
    "How does it impact you when you see me function in my destiny?"

6. Tell Jesus how something impacts your heart.
    "Jesus, when you provide unexpectedly, I feel surprised, joyful—it just makes my heart sing."

7. Take a statement in Scripture, hear it as spoken to you and soak in it. Let the words sink into your heart.
    "Jesus, I receive that as I come to you, you will give you rest."

8. Give thanks for a statement Jesus makes to you that touches your desire.
    "Thank you for putting me at rest, Jesus. I am really grateful for how you touch me."

9. Ask what things are like when desires are filled in heaven.
    "What will it be like to 'shine like the sun' in Father's Kingdom?"

10. Ask for a revelation of who Jesus is.
    "You seem to take special pleasure in blessing people the world ignores. Tell me about that part of you— I want to know you more."

11. Ask what Jesus experienced in a situation from his life.
    "When Peter asked for permission to step out of the boat and walk on water with you, what did you experience in that moment? How were you feeling?"

12. Ask about a feeling Jesus expressed.

    "Jesus, what were you tapping in to when you wept over Jerusalem? What did you see?"

13. Ask one member of the Trinity about another.

    "Jesus, when you see Spirit living in and working through me, what do you love about him?"

14. Identify with the desire of a character in Scripture, and receive Jesus' response to that person out of your identification.

    "The woman caught in adultery—they didn't care about her. They just wanted to use her death to score a political point. I've felt like that. And I love how even though she completely blew it, you put your own life on the line to save her. What made you do that for her and for me?"

LOVE, WORTH

Matthew 8:1-3

"When he came down from the mountain, great crowds followed him; and behold, a leper came to him and knelt before him, saying, 'Lord, if you will, you can make me clean.' And he stretched out his hand and touched him, saying, 'I will; be clean.' And immediately his leprosy was cleansed."

The question is poignant: "…if you will…?" In other words, he was saying, "Master, you can do this if you want to—I just don't know if you want to."

That powerful question reveals the longing of this man's heart. 'What I need to know is if you see me and my awful condition, and if you care. Am I important enough that you would help me? Are you a God that can relate to me, who can feel compassion for suffering, or are you a God of rules who expects us to follow them or bear the consequences?'

By law, a leper was "continuously unclean until cured. He had to wear torn clothes, leave his hair unkempt, cover his upper lip, cry 'unclean, unclean!' and live alone outside the camp."[1]

Imagine the scene: this half-crazed, unsanitary guy comes straight toward Jesus, yelling, 'Unclean! Unclean!' A ripple of fear and loathing passes through the crowd, and people scramble to avoid touching or getting close to the ugly, fearsome disease. Everything about his situation is humiliating, and it all communicates that he is unapproved, untouchable, bad.

He comes to Jesus, his eyes pleading louder than his words. *Does God want anything to do with a screwed up life like mine?* his heart asks. *The law says I am to be banished from God's people for life. Is there anything more for me than to live in lifelong scorn and isolation while my body literally rots away before my eyes?*

Then Jesus reaches out and touches him.

A sharp gasp rises from the crowd. You didn't touch a leper! The disease was contagious, as was the uncleanness. Jesus became ritually unclean—contagious himself—simply by touching him. He broke God's own rule to tell the leper who God really was.

It was a fearless, desire-filling gesture. How many years had it been since anyone outside the leper community touched him? What was it like to be unable to caress his wife, or play with his kids, or hug his parents? To be banished from his town and his faith? To a man who had endured the total withdrawal of human contact, who ached for a touch, that's what Jesus gave—and that touch restored the experience of human contact to his whole life.

Jesus' touch spoke to the deep desire in the man: "I will; be clean. I am a God who sees you, and loves you, and desires to help you. I would break my own rules for you. You are worthy of my attention, and if anyone doubts it, here's the proof: you are healed."

1. *"Jesus, tell me how I am clean today in you."*

2. *"Jesus, would you break the rules for me?"*

3. *"Daddy, here is a place in my heart where I know you can touch me—but sometimes I wonder if you want to. What are you saying to me there today?"*

4. *"Jesus, if we were face-to-face, what would you want to say to me with a physical touch?"*

5. *"Jesus, where in my life do I keep telling myself I am unclean, where you say I am clean already?"*

---

1   International Standard Bible Encyclopedia

JOURNAL

RECOGNITION, CHALLENGE

Matthew 8:5-13

"As Jesus entered the village of Capernaum, a Roman captain came up in a panic and said, 'Master, my servant is sick. He can't walk. He's in terrible pain.' Jesus said, 'I'll come and heal him.' 'Oh, no,' said the captain. 'I don't want to put you to all that trouble. Just give the order and my servant will be fine. I'm a man who takes orders and gives orders. I tell one soldier, 'Go,' and he goes; to another, 'Come,' and he comes; to my slave, 'Do this,' and he does it.' Taken aback, Jesus said, 'I've yet to come across this kind of simple trust in Israel, the very people who are supposed to know all about God and how he works. This man is the vanguard of many outsiders who will soon be coming from all directions—streaming in from the east, pouring in from the west, sitting down at God's kingdom banquet alongside Abraham, Isaac, and Jacob. Then those who grew up 'in the faith' but had no faith will find themselves out in the cold, outsiders to grace and wondering what happened.' Then Jesus turned to the captain and said, 'Go. What you believed could happen has happened.' At that moment his servant became well." (MSG)

In the face of a great challenge, the Roman captain shows remarkable faith. Astonished, Jesus begins to extoll him to the crowd—in all of Israel, he has not come across this kind of simple trust! This man, who was undoubtedly despised for being an officer in the oppressive Roman regime, hailed by Jesus as the forerunner of many who will get a seat at the banquet table of the kingdom! Where the Jews see a despised Gentile, Jesus sees greatness.

This small but profound moment made the centurion a hero of the Bible. This officer did not perceive the greatness of his faith. It just made practical sense to him that if the commander, Jesus, gave the word, it would be done. But Jesus' perspective was far different, for he saw the bigger picture—the story that moment of faith would bring to the world.

Many times we rush by the seemingly-small faith moments in our lives, when Jesus wants to celebrate us for what we've done. Things like remaining faithful in the midst of a personal storm, holding in hurtful words and turning them to prayers when we are wounded, offering a helping hand, or doing a small act of kindness that encourages a heart—these are moments that will be hailed in heaven. Sometimes our greatest moments of faith are when we simply hold on and believe in what the Father has promised in the face of great difficulties.

Jesus loves to recognize our faithfulness in the midst of the challenges of our lives. It's part of seeing our lives from his perspective and letting his love affirm us in the place where we need it most.

1. *"Jesus, what about me today makes you proud?"*

2. *"Spirit, how do you see greatness in how I am navigating my current challenges?"*

3. *"Papa, as we reflect together on my life, what do you want to recognize me for?"*

4. *"Jesus, if you could give me a title that reflects how you see me, what would that title be?"* (For instance mighty warrior, gentle lover, faithful friend.)

5. *"Papa, when I look back at some of the difficulties I've encountered, I often remember my failures and lack. What is your point of view on what I've been through?"*

JOURNAL

JOY, FREEDOM

Matthew 9:2-7 (also Mark 2:1-12)

"And they brought to Him a paralytic lying on a bed. Seeing their faith, Jesus said to the paralytic, 'Take courage, son; your sins are forgiven.' And some of the scribes said to themselves, 'This fellow blasphemes.' And Jesus knowing their thoughts said, 'Why are you thinking evil in your hearts? Which is easier, to say, 'Your sins are forgiven,' or to say, 'Get up, and walk'? 'But so that you may know that the Son of Man has authority on earth to forgive sins'—then He said to the paralytic, 'Get up, pick up your bed and go home.' And he got up and went home."

This passage is a perfect example of how to receive a word of life from Jesus: just come, expecting to get something. That's all. As Hebrews puts it, "He who comes to God must believe that he is, and that he is a rewarder of those who seek him" (Matthew 11:6). I love Mark's version of this story. Jesus was 'at home' (his own place? Peter's? A rental?), with a crowd so thickly packed into the house to hear him that no one could even get through the door. They simply came, expecting to get something.

Out of love for a friend, four men went to a paralytic's home and carried their fellow villager on his bed to Jesus. "Being unable to get to Him because of the crowd, they removed the roof above Him; and when they had dug an opening, they let down the pallet on which the paralytic was lying" (Matthew 2:4). They came, serious about expecting to get something.

A roof in those days would have been fairly flat, its supporting beams covered in branches with layers of plaster or compacted dirt smoothed on top. Inside the house, a commotion starts to drown out the teacher. Dust drifts from the ceiling, then a few pieces of plaster fall, drawing nervous glances. Suddenly, chunks of dirt and plaster shower down all over the protesting crowd. Light streams into the choking fog of dust as the last layer of the roof is torn away. A shouted call from above is answered by the crowd, the light momentarily blocked, and then a broken man on a stretcher is levered through the hole.

Cradled on his neighbor's dirty shoulders, the embarrassed man turns his head away from the crowd—and comes face-to-face with the prophet. Anxious, expectant, ashamed—his mind races, but no words come. Then Jesus reaches out, gently brushes a chunk of plaster from his hair, and smiles. "Cheer up, son! Your sins are forgiven."

So take courage. You aren't a broken body, soul or spirit—you are a son or daughter of your Father in heaven, a brother and sister to Jesus. Jesus would be happy to see you even if you had torn apart the roof above his head to get to him. Come, and discover that everywhere you failed is forgiven and gone. And Jesus is smiling at you.

1. *"Jesus, I've come, expecting to get something. How are you touching my desire today?"*

2. *"Jesus, I long to feel clean, approved, and accepted. How do you see me today?"*

3. *"How am I forgiven, Jesus? Help me understand that more deeply."*

4. *"Jesus, what were you thinking when those guys destroyed the ceiling and rained dirt on you to get into the house? What was going through your mind at that moment?"*

5. *"Let's celebrate our relationship! What do you want to do together today?"*

JOURNAL

APPROVAL, PEACE

Mark 5:25-34 (also Matthew 9:20-22)

"And there was a woman who had had a flow of blood for twelve years, and who had suffered much under many physicians, and had spent all that she had, and was no better but rather grew worse. She had heard the reports about Jesus, and came up behind him in the crowd and touched his garment. For she said, 'If I touch even his garments, I shall be made well.' And immediately the hemorrhage ceased; and she felt in her body that she was healed of her disease. And Jesus, perceiving in himself that power had gone forth from him, immediately turned about in the crowd, and said, 'Who touched my garments?' And his disciples said to him, 'You see the crowd pressing around you, and yet you say, 'Who touched me?'" And he looked around to see who had done it. But the woman, knowing what had been done to her, came in fear and trembling and fell down before him, and told him the whole truth. And he said to her, 'Daughter, your faith has made you well; go in peace, and be healed of your disease.'" (RSV)

When Jesus began looking for who touched him, the woman's heart sank to her toes. He knew. She had violated the rule, again. *You idiot!* Her bleeding made her ritually unclean, and anyone she touched became unclean. Yet her longing to be rid of that 12 years' curse of suffering was so powerful that she took the risk, and actually touched the prophet.

She hadn't wanted anyone to know she was there—that's why she touched his clothes instead of asking to be healed. She didn't even attempt to graze his skin—just the fringe of his robe, trying to keep her shame and dirtiness as far from him as possible. Then she could go home and be rid of this curse forever, and live a normal life. No one would ever know. So she dared the forbidden thing and secretly touched Jesus—and now she was found out.

Jesus' eyes scanned over the crowd, looking for her, as renewed shame washed over her. Her bleeding wasn't just a disease of the body—it was a curse on the soul, and a communicable one at that. And this time she had infected God's anointed.

She believed in Jesus' power to heal, so she also believed he would inevitably discover her—she couldn't hide from the judgment she deserved. So she gulped and stepped forward, afraid to look in his eyes, literally shaking with fear. In a quavering voice she told him everything, the whole shocked crowd listening, then braced herself to endure another brick in the wall of rejection she'd experienced for years.

But to her amazement, Jesus smiled at her, called her daughter, even said, "*your* faith has made you well…" Instead of rejection, she received acceptance; instead of shame, honor; instead of punishment, peace.

1. *Think of a memory where you felt rejected or shamed. Then receive what Jesus says to the woman as if said to you: "Go in peace, and be freed from your suffering."*

2. *"Jesus, where has my faith made something happen? Where are you proud of me for believing?"*

3. *"What was in your heart when you looked for the person who was healed? Why was it important to you to find her?"*

4. *"Jesus, when you healed the woman, you felt it in yourself—power went out from you. Did that drain you? How did it affect you on the days when you healed person after person after person?"*

5. *"Jesus, an area I feel ashamed about is _____. It is hard to come to you like this, but here I am. How do you want to touch me right now?"*

JOURNAL

GOODNESS

Matthew 9:27-30

"As Jesus went on from there, two blind men followed Him, crying out, 'Have mercy on us, Son of David!' When He entered the house, the blind men came up to Him, and Jesus said to them, 'Do you believe that I am able to do this?' They said to Him, 'Yes, Lord.' Then He touched their eyes, saying, 'It shall be done to you according to your faith.' And their eyes were opened."

Jesus' band walked deliberately down the dusty road, the village crowd swirling around him. As the men respectfully asked the teacher questions and children raced happily around this wonderful diversion, two familiar voices began crying out from the back of the group.

The village beggars, unable to work and dependent for their daily bread on the kindness of others, kept calling, "Have mercy on us, Son of David!" Everyone in the crowd had heard this plea often over the years—"have mercy on us!"—and most had supplied a meal or even a coin or two in reply. Although the villagers pitied the men, knowing how difficult their lives were, their actions still betrayed what the law taught: that their blindness was due to sin.

As Jesus entered the home where he was staying, the crowd at last began to disperse. But instead of wandering away, the blind men reached the door, fumbled momentarily with the latch and invaded the house, unbidden, led only by the sound of his voice in their ever-present darkness. "Have mercy on us, Son of David!"

Finally they stood before him, waiting to see what he would do. Eager yet ashamed, they hadn't yet dared to voice their request.

Jesus spoke before they could. "Do you really believe I can do this?"

An electric jolt of adrenalin coursed through them. So he meant to pursue their deepest desire, to be healed, instead of merely offering a meal! "Yes, Lord!" they replied gratefully.

Then, to men who felt their lives had been ruined by some unknown sin they'd committed, whom the law said bore the responsible for their own blindness and poverty, Jesus said, "It shall be done to you according to *your* faith."

They trembled for the briefest moment, replaying the root lie of their lives, that the affliction they lived under was exactly what their sinfulness deserved. *And then they saw!*

And in every moment for the rest of their lives, they experienced the unmistakable evidence of their acceptableness to God: their eyesight.

1. *"Jesus, here's something I deeply desire that I haven't even had the courage to ask for: _____ ."*

2. *"What was going on in your heart when these two guys started calling after you on the dusty road? What were you anticipating?"*

3. *"Jesus, where do you get the grace to keep giving us so much more than we deserve?"*

4. *"What did you see in these two men that caused you to accept them? How do you see that in me?"*

5. *"Jesus, what have you done for me because of my faith?"*

JOURNAL

_____

_____

_____

_____

_____

_____

_____

_____

_____

_____

_____

_____

_____

_____

_____

_____

_____

_____

_____

_____

_____

_____

_____

TO BE KNOWN, VALUE

Matthew 10:29-31

"Are not two sparrows sold for a penny? And not one of them will fall to the ground without your Father's will. But even the hairs of your head are all numbered. Fear not, therefore; you are of more value than many sparrows."

What a picture of being known: that Father has numbered the individual hairs on your head! Take a minute or two and try to count the follicles on the back of your hand. It isn't easy to keep them straight, but Father knows each one.

A sparrow in Jesus' day sold for less money than the smallest coin, and yet they are valuable enough to Father that he pays attention to the fate of every one. Not only that, but each of those commonest of birds has a place in his will and his plan!

Have you ever driven down the same road for a year, and one day noticed a house you'd never seen before, or a sign you missed, or an interesting tree that had never caught your eye before? Our lives are defined by selective perception—we don't even consciously register most of what our senses pick up. I look out my office window every day, but I would be hard-pressed to sketch the scene accurately. Because our mental resources are finite, we have to ignore the vast majority of the details or our brains will go on overload.

Father is not like that. He is infinite, so his perception is infinite. He registers *everything*, sees and remembers it all in full detail. While we must choose to focus on an object to consciously perceive it, he can't *not* see (unless he intentionally chooses to do so). We can know about children dying in Africa or men lost in our prison system, and forget them as soon as they are out of sight—but God cannot. He attends to everything and everyone, always.

And with that infinite perception comes an infinite sense of value. Father sees and knows everything about a bird, a head of hair, or *you,* and seeing it fully he is constantly aware of its true value and loves it fully.

So do not fear. You are known by your Father, fully known in each moment. And you are so valuable to him there is no question that he will look out for you.

1. *"Jesus, you said that Father had the individual hairs on my head numbered. Does he just like counting stuff, or does it come naturally to someone who knows everything? I'd like to know more about this part of you."*

2. *"Papa, what does it give you to fully know me? What does that touch in you?"*

3. *"Give me a picture just for me, so that I can understand how valuable am I to you."*

4. *"How does it impact you when I wonder if my life is worthwhile, or if I'm valuable, or if I am ever going to live up to my destiny?"*

5. *"Father, I know you see everything and love it all—but that is very hard for me to grasp. Give me a little picture of the value of things in your eyes."*

JOURNAL

RECOGNITION

Matthew 10:32

"So everyone who acknowledges me before men, I also will acknowledge before my Father who is in heaven…"

For years I read this passage with mostly fear—or at best, relief. I was afraid that I wasn't a very good evangelist and I might fail this test. Or if I was doing well that week, I'd heave a sigh of relief when I read it, believing that I was going to squeak by. My picture of coming before God was approaching a distant judge, totally alone, waiting for a verdict from an impersonal set of rules that would either free me or imprison me for life.

But this passage gives a totally different picture of what you will experience in heaven. Imagine standing before God, the creator of the universe, for the first time. The book of life is opened, and the saints and angels, the 24 elders and the entire host of heaven wait breathlessly to see what will happen.

Suddenly, at the right hand of God, movement! Jesus rises, walks over next to you and puts his arm around your shoulders.

"This one is mine, Father," he declares, looking back up at the throne. "I'll vouch for her—she's part of the family. Welcome her as you would me."

As all of heaven cheers, Jesus turns to the throng and laughs. "Okay, brothers and sisters, let's show her how we celebrate someone in heaven! Let me tell you the whole story of this amazingly beautiful life, seen through my eyes…"

Your desire to be recognized and to be known will be filled in heaven, on the universe's biggest stage, by the one whose approval means the most.

1. *"Jesus, what is something you want to recognize me for in heaven?"*

2. *"What are you applauding in me today?"*

3. *"Jesus, here's something I'd like to tell all of heaven about you…"*

4. *"How does it touch your heart when we tell others who you are to us here on earth?"*

5. *"What will it be like for you to tell the story of the life we've lived together to all of heaven?"*

JOURNAL

RECOGNITION AND REWARD

Matthew 10:40-42

"He who receives you receives me, and he who receives me receives him who sent me. He who receives a prophet because he is a prophet shall receive a prophet's reward, and he who receives a righteous man because he is a righteous man shall receive a righteous man's reward. And whoever gives to one of these little ones even a cup of cold water because he is a disciple, truly, I say to you, he shall not lose his reward."

Jesus takes heavenly rewards and makes them accessible for everyone. He is talking to people who have done exactly this—they have all received him as a prophet—and says, "you will be rewarded for letting me into your heart—not with just a pat on the head, but with the same reward I get as a

prophet." Just for welcoming him to their village, for listening, for letting him stay in their homes, these people would share in Jesus' inheritance.[2]

Just like them, you will share in Jesus' reward for receiving him into your heart. Not only that, you will not lose your reward for the smallest act of service. Offering to share a stick of gum, opening a door for a man with a cane, holding a crying child with a skinned knee—any little thing you do out of the compassion of Jesus will end up posted on the Wall of the Heroes of Heaven.

The followers of Jesus who are most tuned in to these small acts of kindness often feel overlooked or unrecognized, because they see things others don't. To you, Jesus says, "I will not forget what you've done. Every kind thing you've done for someone you've really done for me, and you will be recognized and celebrated in heaven for each one.

1. *"Jesus, what have I done for someone this week that you will remember?"*

2. *"Give me a picture of how you celebrate some small act of kindness I've done for you."*

3. *"Jesus, how do you feel when you are able to give the prophet's reward to anyone who even listens to you? What does it give you to reward us all out of proportion with what we've done?"*

4. *"Holy Spirit, what do you see and love in Jesus when he is rewarding his people?"*

5. *"Jesus, here is how it impacts me to hear you talk about your reward system…"*

---

2   For more on God's reward system, see the meditation on Matthew 23:11-12 (pages 104 and 106).

JOURNAL

....
....
....
....
....
....
....
....
....
....
....
....
....
....
....
....
....
....
....
....
....
....
....
....
....
....

FREEDOM

Matthew 11:2-6

"When John, who was in prison, heard about the deeds of the Messiah, he sent his disciples to ask him, 'Are you the one who is to come, or should we expect someone else?' Jesus replied, 'Go back and report to John what you hear and see: The blind receive sight, the lame walk, those who have leprosy are cleansed, the deaf hear, the dead are raised, and the good news is proclaimed to the poor. Blessed is anyone who does not stumble on account of me.'" (NIV)

John is the greatest of the prophets, who prepared the way for the Messiah to come. But the one with the highest calling now sits in the lowest circumstances, powerless in a prison cell, while the cousin he promoted is out healing, raising the dead and helping the helpless.

We don't know how much they were around each other as boys, but John did baptize Jesus. He knew then that his cousin carried the greater calling. There, before John's eyes, as Jesus emerged from the water, heaven opened and the Spirit descended on Jesus like a dove, and a voice thundered, "This is my son, whom I love, with whom I am well pleased" (Matthew 3:17).

John knew that Jesus was the Messiah. But the doubts came when he looked at the realities of his earthly situation. Wasn't the Messiah coming to set things right, to set the captives free and to bring the Kingdom of Heaven to earth? It almost seems as if John is saying, "Hey, cous', if you have all that power and calling, could you come set me free?" Or, "If you are who you say you are, could you pay attention over here to my plight?" And maybe, he even wondered, *If this is the way things are going to turn out, are you really who I thought you were?*

When we are focused on our own circumstances, we tend to ask Jesus to get us out of them because we long for freedom *from* our circumstance—a change in the earthly reality we live in. At times, this is just what happens. There is healing or release or dramatic shifts in our situation. We learn to call heaven to earth and miracles come. But not always.

However, there is yet a greater freedom available—even greater than the freedom from our circumstances. It is the freedom *within*. It is the power to experience the goodness of God in the midst of challenge, pain or suffering; the ability to enjoy the freedom of trusting when we do not understand. This is a freedom that no earthly situation can take away. We transcend it through our trust in the relationship, and so receive strength to face the storm and walk through to the other side. We lean into Jesus, and instead of transforming the circumstances, we ourselves are transformed.

Either way, the road we walk with him is a freedom road.

1. *"Papa, what are you delighted to set free within me today?"*

2. *"Spirit, let's remember the times you have shifted my circumstances in answer to my cry. Take me back to one of those memories so we can rejoice in it together!"*

3. *"The times you haven't changed my situation, even though I wanted you to—what is one way you've transformed my heart through trusting you in my circumstances?"*

4. *"Abba, take me in your lap and show me how you feel about what I'm facing or where I've been."*

5. *"Jesus you are the Truth that sets me free. What truth about your character and heart are you showing me right now?"*

JOURNAL

PEACE

Matthew 11:28-30

"Come to me, all who labor and are heavy laden, and I will give you rest. Take my yoke upon you, and learn from me; for I am gentle and lowly in heart, and you will find rest for your souls. For my yoke is easy, and my burden is light. Are you tired? Worn out? Burned out on religion? Come to me. Get away with me and you'll recover your life. I'll show you how to take a real rest. Walk with me and work with me—watch how I do it. Learn the unforced rhythms of grace. I won't lay anything heavy or ill-fitting on you. Keep company with me and you'll learn to live freely and lightly." (MSG)

According to tradition, Jesus in his role as a *tekton* (Greek for carpenter or builder) made yokes and ploughs. Each yoke had to be custom-fitted to each animal. As one yoke-builder notes:

> *"Yokes for oxen are like shoes for children. One size does not fit all. A young team may need as many as five or six yokes before it reaches maturity. A well-fitted yoke will allow an ox team to pull to its full potential. A poorly fitted yoke will cause discomfort, could injure the oxen, and will not allow the team to pull to its full potential."* [3]

When Jesus the master craftsman said "my yoke is easy," memories flooded back to him of his time in the woodshop: carving the curved opening in the yoke to fit around each animal's neck, sanding it down carefully so that it would not rub any spot raw or hurt the animal. When he asks you to, "take my yoke upon you," he means the one he custom-made just for you and him. It's designed to preserve you from unnecessary pain and let you reach your full potential. Just as yokes were made to join the pulling power of two animals, his yoke is meant to join your strength to his and let the two of you to pull together.

1. *"I think I need a yoke refitting. I long for a deep rest for my soul. How do you want to give me a sense of 'easy' and 'light' today as we work together, Jesus?"*

2. *"Jesus, with everything there is to do, it's hard to stay in the easy yoke with you. What do you want to say about all the things on my to-do list today?"*

3. *"How did you do it? How did you maintain such an easy, intimate connection with Father here on earth?"*

4. *"What do you mean when you say you are 'gentle and lowly in heart?' Speak to me that way now—I want to connect with that part of who you are."*

5. *"Jesus, thanks for believing in me when you say, 'you will find rest for your souls.' Honestly, sometimes I wonder if I'm going to make it, and it's just good to know that you believe in me."*

---

3   *Tiller's Tech Guide – Building An Ox Yoke*

JOURNAL

FREEDOM, RECOGNITION

Matthew 13:41-43

"The Son of Man will send forth His angels, and they will gather out of His kingdom all stumbling blocks, and those who commit lawlessness, and will throw them into the furnace of fire; in that place there will be weeping and gnashing of teeth. Then the righteous will shine forth like the sun in the kingdom of their Father. He who has ears, let him hear."

Stumbling blocks, injustice, breaking the rules, temptations—life is full of them. But imagine a place where Father has gathered up all those things we struggle with, and removed them completely. You are free.

In that heaven, you never again have to fight against lust, envy or anger. There is no need to exercise self-control, because only good comes out of yourself, effortlessly and naturally. You'll never again be wounded by another's wound, or crushed by an uncaring system, or hurt yourself with a poor choice. There is nothing to protect your heart against.

Sounds good, doesn't it? That is the place Father has chosen you for, Jesus has built for you, and you will one day walk into.

You are being remade for that every day, in secret. The Kingdom of God growing in you in this parable (see verses 24-30) is hidden in plain sight. Jesus compares you to wheat sprouting in a field an enemy has sabotaged with a plant called darnel. This poisonous middle-eastern weed is virtually indistinguishable from wheat—up until the heads of grain appear.[4] Only then can the weeds and the wheat be separated.

The good and the bad grow up in this world together, and often it is hard to tell them apart. Who can say whether the real truth comes out in court, or in the news, or politics, or even in everyday disagreements at work? Who really knows what glory resides within you?

Who you really are is hidden within a cloud, and only faint wisps of light escape to hint at it. But on God's day, the cloud will be removed, and "those who have insight will shine brightly like the brightness of the expanse of heaven, and those who lead the many to righteousness, like the stars forever and ever" (Daniel 12:3). You will be fully seen, fully known and fully valued, in the glory your life has earned.

"Beloved, we are God's children now. It does not yet appear what we shall be, but we know that when he appears we shall be like him, for we shall see him as he is" (I John 3:2).

1. *Soak in the fact that in heaven, all causes of sin are removed—you're free! You will no longer even be aware of temptation, let alone have to fight it. Let that thought sink into your heart.*

2. *"Jesus, help me picture what it will look like when I 'shine like the sun' in Father's Kingdom"*

3. *"Jesus, I long to be seen, known and valued. When you take the wraps off, the you in me will shine for all to see—but how do you know and value me now?"*

4. *"How do you see me as righteous today? How do I look from your perspective?"*

5. *"What are you feeling when you see us, the people you gave your life for, shining like the sun in Father's Kingdom? What does that touch in your heart?"*

---

4   To sow darnel to sabotage a wheat field was actually a crime in Roman law.

JOURNAL

WORTH

Matthew 13:51-52

"'Have you understood all these things?' Jesus asked. 'Yes,' they replied. He said to them, 'Therefore every teacher of the law who has become a disciple in the kingdom of heaven is like the owner of a house who brings out of his storeroom new treasures as well as old.'"

A way of translating this passage that we can relate to might be, "Every scholar who has also become a student of the Kingdom of Heaven…" Picture a religion professor at a university sitting in the grass on a hillside, listening to Jesus tell stories about heaven. Jesus has a special treasure for those who are learned and can still learn; or those who are fathers in the faith but are still able to become like kids and get something out of story time. Being asked a childlike question always warms your Daddy's heart.

Even when we move on to a new place in our walk with God, Father never stops valuing what we've done in the past. Have you ever entered a new stage in life and then pooh-poohed how you

used to act? Maybe you look back on how you used to think college was such hard work and laugh, or reread an early journal entry and cringe at your naivety, or joke about the crazy things you did as a young Christian. We have a tendency to disparage anything we have moved beyond.

However, *all* of your devotion to God, new or old, done well or done poorly, is of great value to Father. Like parents saving the artwork you did in kindergarten or videotaping your first soccer game, he treasures each encounter with you. Every awkward whiff of a kick or crayon straying outside the lines simply makes the picture more endearing. Every moment spent in pursuit of your Father in heaven is another gem cached in the storerooms of your relationship. He loves all those treasured memories, both old and new.

1. *"Tell me about the storeroom that is in the house of my heart. What do you say is in it?"*

2. *"What is a treasure I have that I can bring to you today?"*

3. *"When I enter a new season or learn a new way of doing life, I tend to look down on where I used to be. Is there a place I've done that where you'd like to show me how you see it?"*

4. *"Father, you seem to take extra delight when we come to you like children—when those who already know you can still be pupils and learn something new. Why does that especially please you?"*

5. *"Father, sometimes I regret all the time I've spent studying rules and biblical principles without really connecting with your heart in them. How is that time valuable to you?"*

JOURNAL

COMFORT, SECURITY

Matthew 14:25-27

"Meanwhile, the boat was far out to sea when the wind came up against them and they were battered by the waves. At about four o'clock in the morning, Jesus came toward them walking on the water. They were scared out of their wits. 'A ghost!' they said, crying out in terror. But Jesus was quick to comfort them. 'Courage, it's me. Don't be afraid.'"(MSG)

Picture the scene. A small wooden boat labors in the black water, pale moonlight glistening off the muscled arms of a tired fisherman, standing upright, wrestling the steering oar. Four oarsmen beat a slow rhythm against the head-wind, showing little progress for a cold night's work. Slumped between the benches, a group of wet-through, sea-sick landlubbers huddle in the bottom of the boat, inert as ballast. Their curses and complaints at their companions' ineptitude have long since tapered off into low moans.

The twelve men set off the night before, trusting the fishermen's assurances that they'd be home by bedtime. Then an unexpected storm blew up. Now bone-tired, cold, frustrated at each other and a little scared, they longed to catch a glimpse of the shore.

Instead, a startled oarsman screamed in terror, spying a ghostly apparition on the water. The gray figure was heading straight for the boat, ignoring the spray. "Look—over there!" the fisherman pointed, crouching behind the gunwale. "God save us! It's a ghost!"

Jesus was quick to comfort them. "Courage— it's me," he shouted, turning slightly to bring his familiar face out of shadow and into the moonlight. "Don't be afraid!"

Although the figure they saw on the water was a great friend, the disciples' memories of fisherman's tales and childhood ghost stories had twisted their vision. Instead of a familiar protector, those memories led them to see danger, and shrink back from Jesus in fear.

Jesus' response was immediate: "Look, it's me! You know me—and you know you have nothing to fear from me."

We share the disciples' experience. Our memories of past failures, hurts and bitter disappointments cause us to react fearfully when Jesus comes to touch the deep waters of our hearts. We need to keep on hearing the voice of the one who yearns to comfort us: "Courage; it's me. Don't be afraid."

1. *"Jesus, sometimes I am afraid that you will _____. Is that true?"*

2. *"Jesus, I have a deep longing for comfort and security. What do you want to say to me there?"*

3. *"Where in my life do you want to say, 'It's me—don't be afraid?'"*

4. *"Jesus, where do you see courage in me?"*

5. *"So what's it like for you to not be afraid of anything?"*

LOVE, SECURITY

Matthew 14:28-32

"And Peter answered him, 'Lord, if it is you, bid me come to you on the water.' He said, 'Come.' So Peter got out of the boat and walked on the water and came to Jesus; but when he saw the wind, he was afraid, and beginning to sink he cried out, 'Lord, save me.' Jesus immediately reached out his hand and caught him, saying to him, 'O man of little faith, why did you doubt?' And when they got into the boat, the wind ceased." (RSV)

I have a hard time visualizing myself having the audaciousness to ask Jesus to walk on water. Okay, let's be honest—there is *no way* I would step out onto a choppy sea out of sight of land and try to walk across the waves. Even beyond the physical act of standing on top of a lake is the impudence of what Peter is asking Jesus to do. "Jesus, *if* this is you, even though you are in the midst of performing a miracle, do another one just for me, just to prove it's really you." I didn't think we were supposed to ask stuff like that.

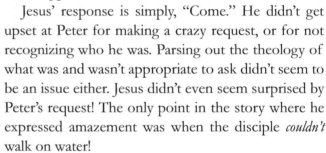

Jesus' response is simply, "Come." He didn't get upset at Peter for making a crazy request, or for not recognizing who he was. Parsing out the theology of what was and wasn't appropriate to ask didn't seem to be an issue either. Jesus didn't even seem surprised by Peter's request! The only point in the story where he expressed amazement was when the disciple *couldn't* walk on water!

You've got to love the direction Peter is going, though. "Bid me come to you…" Peter asks for a miracle to get him closer to Jesus. "If this is really you, Jesus, you'll ask me to get closer, because I know that's what you are about. I'll do this crazy, insane thing if you just say yes, because I know that you'd do whatever it takes to be closer to me."

Even Peter's failure of belief is glorious. He began to doubt whether Jesus could enable him to walk on water—so Jesus reached out, pulled him up and *walked with him on the water back to the boat.* Jesus didn't carry Peter. He didn't throw him back into the boat—they got back in the boat *together.* Even when Peter's faith failed him, Jesus enabled him to do the thing he had asked to do.

What would happen if you were as fearless in your requests today as Peter? What might happen if you asked for a miracle in your life to get you closer to him?

1. *"Jesus, I want to get closer. Bid me come to you in a way that stretches my faith and takes a miracle."*

2. *"Jesus, what am I missing about who you are that makes it hard for me to be as bold as Peter?"*

3. *"When Peter was in trouble, you immediately reached out and rescued him. What are you already working to rescue me from today?"*

4. *"You did for Peter what he couldn't do for himself. How are you doing that for me?"*

5. *"Jesus, I often feel like I'm sitting in the boat, watching others take leaps of faith that I'm too scared to attempt. I feel like I'm such a slow learner in this. How do you feel about my progress?"*

JOURNAL

WORTH, SECURITY

Matthew 15:25-28

"But she came and began to bow down before Him, saying, 'Lord, help me!' And He answered and said, 'It is not good to take the children's bread and throw it to the dogs.' But she said, 'Yes, Lord; but even the dogs feed on the crumbs which fall from their masters' table.' Then Jesus said to her, 'O woman, your faith is great; it shall be done for you as you wish.' And her daughter was healed at once."

This story is about asking for the wrong thing at the wrong time in the wrong way, and how Jesus responds. Jesus' mission was not to minister to Gentile women: that work was reserved for his body, the church, after his return to heaven. She made the wrong request. And to do it, she interrupted a private get-away Jesus had arranged just for himself and his disciples. He had finally left the country altogether to escape the constant demands of the crowds, and then he was confronted by this crazy woman who wouldn't leave well enough alone. It was the wrong time.

On top of that, the woman made a nuisance of herself, "bothering" the disciples and "driving us crazy" (MSG). Even though his gatekeepers said "no," she wouldn't stop. Ignoring them, she went over their heads and took her case straight to Jesus, begging him on her knees for help. Rude and invasive, she made her request in the wrong way.

So how did Jesus respond to this woman's inappropriate request, made at the wrong time, in a rude, demanding way? He commended her faith and broke all the rules to give her her desire! How deep, how wide, how high is his yearning to help us when we are in trouble! Even when it was outside of his purpose, the timing was wrong, and the way she asked was annoying and abrasive, Jesus reached out to rescue her and protect a daughter he had never even met. How much more will he long to answer your prayers and fill the deepest desires of your heart!

Take a place in life where you feel ashamed to keep asking for help, and put yourself into this story. Jesus delighted in the fact that she kept asking and never gave up on her belief that he was good and he would be good to her. His heart is the same toward you.

1. *"Jesus, where I feel the least worthy of being touched by you is _____. What do you love about me there?"*

2. *"Father, sometimes I'm embarrassed to keep asking you for _____. What do you like about it when I keep on bringing this to you and don't give up?"*

3. *"Father, how are you protecting me today?"*

4. *"Daddy, hold me in your big, strong arms and tell me how I am safe in you."*

5. *"Holy Spirit, tell me about your name, 'The Helper'. What do you like about helping me?"*

JOURNAL

SECURITY, BEING KNOWN

Matthew 15:32

"But Jesus wasn't finished with them. He called his disciples and said, 'I hurt for these people. For three days now they've been with me, and now they have nothing to eat. I can't send them away without a meal—they'd probably collapse on the road.'" (MSG)

"And Jesus called His disciples to Him, and said, 'I feel compassion for the people, because they have remained with Me now three days and have nothing to eat; and I do not want to send them away hungry, for they might faint on the way.'"

After three days together, camping out on the mountainside in front of a beautiful view of the lake, Jesus felt bonded to the people. He'd taught the group, healed many individuals one at a time and rejoiced with them as they responded to Father's touch. Over the three days, he'd sat around their campfires, shared their stories and conversed with many of them one-on-one. But now it was time to go.

He was drawn to them by deep compassion, and that same care led to his concern about what they would experience on the long walk home. Watching them at mealtimes, he realized that many had simply dropped everything and come, wanting so badly to be touched by God that they hadn't thought to bring provisions for even a day, let alone three.

Jesus was proud of how the people had responded. They'd become a true community, sharing freely and welcoming those who had nothing to join their family circles. No one went hungry for those three days, as joy and laughter rang out from a hundred little circles around the cooking fires.

"This is just what I wanted, Father," Jesus whispered, gazing over the little groups scattered across the hillside. "They are treating each other the way we do. Loving, sharing everything, honoring each other—what a beautiful picture of our fellowship. Seeing you in them fills me, Father—I am truly satisfied with what we have accomplished."

And yet, seeing them munching their last stale crusts stirred Jesus to action. They had done well, sharing what they had: now Father would multiply their efforts beyond what was humanly possible, until the entire need was met. He saw their need, and he touched it.

Jesus miraculously multiplied the few leftovers so his family wouldn't have to travel home on an empty stomach. But his actions spoke a larger message: that what we begin out of love for him, he will move heaven and earth to finish.

1. *"Jesus, thank you for providing for me so well. Thank you for food and water and the simple things you supply for life every day."*

2. *"Tell me how you are aware of me today, Jesus. What in my life has your attention?"*

3. *"Jesus, what are you proud of in me today? How am I filling your desire?"*

4. *"Jesus, show your compassion for someone I love. How is that person on your heart today?"*

5. *"Jesus, I just ran after you without planning for the journey. What's one way you provided for me, so I wouldn't faint along the way?"*

JOURNAL

BEING KNOWN

Matthew 16:15-19

"He pressed them, 'And how about you? Who do you say I am?' Simon Peter said, 'You're the Christ, the Messiah, the Son of the living God.' Jesus came back, 'God bless you, Simon, son of Jonah! You didn't get that answer out of books or from teachers. My Father in heaven, God himself, let you in on this secret of who I really am. And now I'm going to tell you who you are, really are. You are Peter, a rock. This is the rock on which I will put together my church, a church so expansive with energy that not even the gates of hell will be able to keep it out.' And that's not all. You will have complete and free access to God's kingdom, keys to open any and every door: no more barriers between heaven and earth, earth and heaven. A yes on earth is yes in heaven. A no on earth is no in heaven.'" (MSG)

Hanging around Jesus taught his disciples to know and name each other's true identities. From Nathan, "an Israelite indeed, in whom there is no guile" (John 1:47) to James and John, the "sons of thunder" (Mark 3:17), Jesus called out what was in each individual in his inner circle.

"Who do you say I am?" is an invitation for the disciples to do the same for their leader. Jesus starts by asking who the crowds say that he is—who he appears to be on the outside, to those who don't know him intimately. Then he asks for more from his disciples—"Now, you who really know me—tell me who I really am."

Peter rises to the occasion, replying, "You're the Christ, the Messiah, the Son of God." What a beautiful moment for Jesus, when one of his closest friends touches his deep desire to be known for who he really is! And what a glorious moment for his church, as Jesus' followers learned to look beyond surface impressions and call out a person's true identity.

Jesus keeps the life flowing by turning around and telling Peter who he really is. "Happy are you, Simon son of Jonah," Jesus exults. "You got it. Not just knowing who I am, but taking the risk of speaking to my deepest desire and true identity. And you did it out of how Father sees me, instead of settling for how I look to the crowds on the outside. Keep doing this! Keep on saying 'yes!' to who people really are, and you will truly be blessed."

1. *"Who do you say that I am, Jesus?"*

2. *"Jesus, how did it impact you when someone finally called out your true identity?"*

3. *"Jesus, I want to return the favor: here's who you really are to me."*

4. *"Tell me about having 'complete and free access to God's Kingdom'. What does that give me?"*

5. *"Jesus, who could we surprise by telling them who they really are today?"*

JOURNAL

LOVE

Matthew 17:5

"While he was still speaking, a bright cloud overshadowed them, and behold, a voice out of the cloud said, 'This is my beloved Son, with whom I am well-pleased; listen to Him!'"

This is a passage to steep your heart in. As Jesus often put it, "let these words sink into your heart." As you read, instead of thinking about the theological implications of the passage, simply let Father's words impact you. He is speaking the same thing to you now as he did on that day 2000 years ago. "You are beloved forever. You are adopted into my family. I am pleased with you."

Taste that truth; let it be a living reality that enters you and affects your being. Let love wrap around you and hold your heart in its embrace. Be within Father's arms, like a child experiencing the warmth and security of being held. Let the wordless experience of being his flood over and fill you to overflowing.

To truly know, the heart must experience truth. To truly experience, the heart must open and embrace the mystery of a touch that supersedes understanding. When right knowledge *about* the Trinity is mated with experiential truth *in* them—a truth tasted and seen and touched—then we can truly say we know the Father, Son and Spirit.

1. *Allow Father to speak these words to you, and let them sink into your heart: "You are my beloved son [or daughter]; in you I am well-pleased."*

2. *"Father, how am I swept up into your love in this moment?"*

3. *"Daddy, what makes you happy with me today? How are you exulting over me?"*

4. *"Father, tell me about your love for Jesus."*

5. *"Daddy, just let me look in your loving eyes this morning. I don't need any words—just to look on you is enough."*

SIGNIFICANCE, ACHIEVEMENT

Matthew 17:20

"Then the disciples came to Jesus privately and said, 'Why could we not drive it out?' And He said to them, 'Because of the littleness of your faith; for truly I say to you, if you have faith the size of a mustard seed, you will say to this mountain, 'Move from here to there,' and it will move; and nothing will be impossible to you.'"

Think for a moment about the context of this passage where Jesus declares that his disciples' faith was tiny (we'll refer to Luke because it is the most chronological of the gospels). These guys had just been out traveling the nation healing the sick "everywhere" (Luke 9:6). Only nine days before they had heard Peter's great confession (Luke 9:20) and Jesus' reply that, "Whatever you bind on earth is bound in heaven." They were feeling it. And they were acting fully empowered by

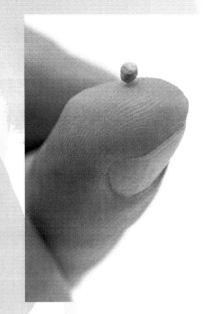

carrying on Jesus' ministry while he took a day off to retreat on the mountain (Luke 9:28). That's when the story of the epileptic takes place.

So in the midst of being released into their destiny in ministry, of doing amazing miracles that would have been inconceivable to them a year before, Jesus calls them to something larger. "All that you've done so far—healing the sick, casting out demons, preaching the good news? That's small potatoes. Just a tiny amount of faith was sufficient for that. You've run up against the limits of your belief in this case, but you need to understand—God is so, so much bigger than you believe he is. In fact, if your tiny faith grew even to the size of a mustard seed, you could do anything—anything! If you really understood how big my Father is, and believed it, nothing would be impossible for you."

If your deep desire is to lead a significant life, to change the world, Jesus is speaking to your heart. "Nothing will be impossible for you!"

Your destiny is based on what you believe. It isn't about how intelligent you are, or whether you have money, or opportunity, or if you were born into privilege. If you have even a little faith, no person or circumstance can stop you from becoming who you were born to be. You run around with a great big God, and you can do great big things.

1. *"Father, how am I significant to you today?"*

2. *"Jesus, what have you already accomplished with my faith that you are really proud of?"*

3. *"Daddy, what's something I can use my faith on today?"*

4. *"Jesus, what's one thing that looks like an impossible challenge to me that you say we can tackle together?"*

5. *"Father, I'm going to stretch myself and ask for something really big, because I believe in you and you are good. Here it is: _____."*

JOURNAL

BEING KNOWN, SECURITY

Matthew 18:10

"See that you do not despise one of these little ones, for I say to you that their angels in heaven continually see the face of My Father who is in heaven."

"Watch that you don't treat a single one of these childlike believers arrogantly. You realize, don't you, that their personal angels are constantly in touch with my Father in heaven?" (MSG)

In this famous 1963 photo, President John F. Kennedy's son John Jr. is shown playing under the famous Resolute desk in the oval office. Born in the White House, John Jr. called the kneehole behind his secret door "my house." To him, the leader of 250 million people was simply "Daddy," and the nerve center of the country was his play place.

In the same way, "our house" is the nerve center of a kingdom, and our joys and concerns go straight to the top. As children of the king, our personal ambassador-angels enjoy constant face-time with Father. Heaven actually has a communication system in place to keep the smallest need of the youngest toddler from being overlooked!

When we think of access to a President, we envision a line of aides waiting at his door, each ushered in for a few precious minutes to deal with their agenda. But as sons, we have a secret door to a playground under the throne of heaven. Even while orchestrating the business of the universe, Father has an infinite number of moments to spend thinking of *you*. Not only are the hairs on your head numbered, but each one is tracked daily, and his count changes every time even one falls out!

And this amazing Father talks down to no one. The word "despise" in this verse means "to think little of" or "look down on." The reason we are commanded to look down on no one is because that's how Father treats us. Everyone who approaches him is fully worthy of his time and fully engages his attention. No one is looked down on.

Right now, Father is receiving up-to-the-minute reports on your joys and concerns. Your personal representative has an audience with him this very moment. He fully knows you, constantly looks out for you—and the secret door to playing under the throne is always open.

1. *"Jesus, what does it look like when the angel representatives have an audience with Father?"*

2. *"Father, how would you like me to think of heaven as 'my house?'"*

3. *"How would you like me to play under your throne today, Papa?"*

4. *"Father, how do you pay attention to all of us at the same time? I have a hard time staying focused on even one thing!"*

5. *"Father, my desire is to be fully known. Let me experience how I am fully known by you today."*

JOURNAL

BELONGING, COMFORT

Matthew 18:19-20

"When two of you get together on anything at all on earth and make a prayer of it, my Father in heaven goes into action. And when two or three of you are together because of me, you can be sure that I'll be there." (MSG)

An ancient Jewish saying attributed to a rabbi of Jesus' day was, "But [when] two sit together and there are words of Torah [spoken] between them, the Divine Presence rests with them…" In this passage, Jesus states that he himself is the *Shekinah*, the divine presence that rests between his followers. That's pretty cool. When two Christians get together to talk about Jesus, he is right there in the conversation. And even cooler: the Jews of that time believed that talking about God's *rules* was what caused God to show up. However, Jesus told his best friends on earth that anytime they talked about *him*, he'd be right there with them. Instead of meeting Father when we talk rules and principles, in Jesus' economy we meet him when we talk family.

For this to really hit home, you have to put yourself in the situation of the people Jesus was addressing. He was talking to the band that ate with him, slept on the ground with him, chatted together on the on the long hours on the road. The disciples were like a rock band on tour together for three solid years. That's a lot of togetherness!

My own first experience of feeling fully known was in a worship band I traveled with for several years. They knew me at my best and my worst. They experienced my spiritual sensitivity and my inability to read music, my crazy sense of humor and my maddening tendency to go off key—and they loved me in all of it. I felt I could be totally myself with that group and it was okay.

To a tight group like that, more attached to him than anyone else, Jesus says, "I am going to die soon. Where I'm going you can't come, and you are going to miss me. But even though I am leaving, I am not going to leave you alone! Anytime you get together and talk about me, I will be there with you. I'm not talking about just as a fond memory, but *actually, really there:* a divine presence entering your conversation, talking with you."

The glory of God—the holy, *Shekinah* presence that filled Solomon's temple but was conspicuously absent from Herod's—was to come back and dwell on earth again. But this time it wouldn't be on rules, or even on buildings, but on the fellowship of as few as two ordinary believers. Amazing!

1. *"Jesus, help me understand this presence thing. What's a picture I can grasp of how you are there when we talk about you?"*

2. *"Jesus, thanks for not leaving us alone—I'm grateful. Why was that so important to you?"*

3. *"Papa, how have you gone into action because of a prayer I've shared in this week?"*

4. *"How do you want to be present in my conversations today?"*

5. *"Why are you especially present when two of us talk about you, versus when it is just you and me?"*

JOURNAL

WORTH

Matthew 19:13-15

"One day children were brought to Jesus in the hope that he would lay hands on them and pray over them. The disciples shooed them off. But Jesus intervened: 'Let the children alone, don't prevent them from coming to me. God's kingdom is made up of people like these.'" (MSG)

The disciples were having a rough time that day, trying to play gatekeeper for Jesus and screen out the people who weren't really worth his time. But the criteria for admission were different than what they assumed. Jesus repeatedly broke the rules about who got in to see the great Teacher, usually on behalf of those society deemed less worthwhile (women and children), sinful (the woman who washed his feet) or even untouchable (the lepers). The disciples never seemed to grasp that the people they saw as least likely to merit Jesus' attention were the ones most assured of getting it.

It doesn't matter whether you are old or young, with the 'in' crowd or a stoner, a geek or captain of the football team: Jesus sees incredible value in you. You are an individual he lovingly hand-crafted and then died for—worth far more than human society believes.

The disciples tried to bar the children's access because they saw them as less valuable, believing that they needed to grow up and have serious questions and responsibilities to be worthy of Jesus' time. But Jesus replies, "These children don't need to become more like grown-ups to hang around me. They are always welcome—in fact, my house is full of them. It wouldn't hurt you to be more like children instead of the other way around."

So often we try too hard to act all grown up for Jesus. We decide what we 'ought to know by now' and take it on ourselves to do it. We make little rules about what questions are and aren't appropriate to ask God, or what emotions we can and can't express to him. It's easy to fall into the same trap as the disciples and function as our own little gatekeepers, trying to filter what we bring to God so we're sure it is worth his attention.

Jesus is saying, "Hey, Papa and I don't need you to act all grown-uppity and try to manage us. And we don't need you to filter yourself around us, either—all of you is welcome here! You can come to Papa like a child any time and say, 'Bless me, Daddy!' or, 'It really hurts,' or even, 'I'm mad at you.' My friendship and Pap's lap are always available."

Father's Kingdom is not a big adult world, where you are responsible for everything on your plate by yourself. Even the smallest concerns of a child are his concerns.

1. *"Jesus, how do you want to lay your hands on me and bless me today?"*

2. *"What's one way that I can be less grown-uppity and more like a kid with you today that you'd really enjoy?"*

3. *"Jesus, my longing is to feel less weight of responsibility and more rest and peace. So here's my pile of cares. How do you want to touch me there?"*

4. *"How am I valuable to you? What makes me worth your time and attention?"*

5. *"Jesus, what are you praying over me right now?"*

JOURNAL

SIGNIFICANCE, RECOGNITION

Matthew 19:27-29

"Peter answered him, 'We have left everything to follow you! What then will there be for us?' Jesus said to them, 'I tell you the truth, at the renewal of all things, when the Son of man sits on his glorious throne, you who have followed me will also sit on twelve thrones, judging the twelve tribes of Israel.'"

This conversation comes on the heels of Jesus' dialogue with the rich young ruler. The disciples are simultaneously astonished and discouraged to hear Jesus say a rich person getting into heaven was like squeezing a camel through the tiny hole in a needle. It flew in the face of their Jewish culture! For their entire lives they had embraced a belief Jesus was now challenging: *riches are a sign of God's approval, his blessing.*

This motley band of 12 had set aside jobs and careers to participate in an anything-goes-internship with Jesus. Their old clients had moved on to former competitors. Now unemployed and

living off a common purse of donations from Jesus' followers, they were committed whether they liked it or not. They had all their eggs in one basket.

I don't see Peter as having entitlement issues or trying to make a power play. He had a lot of *chutzpah*, willing—or maybe impulsive—enough to say what others would only think. I can imagine the disciples holding their collective breath, all eyes on Jesus, wondering how he would respond to Peter's blunt question: "What's in this for us?"

Undaunted by Peter's audacity, Jesus looks beyond the surface and speaks to his deep desire. Peter is not after money—his true longing is to lead a significant life, and to be recognized for the challenging sacrifices he had made. Jesus directly addresses that desire: "Your sacrifice will be recognized in heaven, and you will be honored with a significant role. Don't be afraid that you'll miss out for investing in this one thing: the life you've chosen to lead won't just change the world; it will change heaven, too!"

Jesus was not skittish about telling the disciples what was in it for them. Graciously, he gives them a glimpse of the instrumental part they would be rewarded with in eternity. And his words stirred their hearts with hope—and with reassurance that their investment in heaven was secure.

1. *"Jesus, I'll take a risk and ask Peter's question: 'What's in this for me?'"*

2. *"What will it be like when we rule gloriously together?"*

3. *"Jesus, how is my life significant in your Kingdom?"*

4. *"What do you love about how I've invest my life in following you?"*

5. *"Jesus, I long to have an impact in your Kingdom. Show me the way you work so I can live the way I was made to live."*

JOURNAL

COMFORT

Matthew 19:29

"And everyone who has left houses or brothers or sisters or father or mother or children or farms for my name's sake, will receive many times as much, and will inherit eternal life. But many who are first will be last; and the last, first."

His final day on the job was bittersweet. The light was fading as he hung the last of the tools on the back wall, then brushed the cedar shavings from the scarred workbench. Tossing his leather apron aside, he ran his hand over the thick wood, remembering—the rhythm of the saw, the bite of a well-sharpened chisel, the laughter as he and his brothers hammered out a door or an ox yoke for a neighbor.

A last supper awaited with his family next door, his clan for all of his 30 years. A final night of sleep on the roof under the stars, and tomorrow he'd walk out the door for good.

"My last day," Jesus breathed, looking over the shop one final time as if to capture every detail. He closed his eyes, breathing deeply the pungent cedar aroma and sweet smell of pine sap, then stepped out into the cooling air and walked the few steps back to his ancestral home. The anticipation of what Father would do was great, but the sorrow was as well. He was going to miss his family, his hometown, and the carpenter's shop.

Jesus knows the sweet sorrow of moving on, of missing of loved ones and special places. He experienced the real pain of leaving things behind to follow God's call. The greater leaving for him was to put off his divine nature, leave heaven and put on a human body to come live with us. Knowing the cost of leaving his home and family for our sake, he reserves a special glory for those of us who leave something behind for his.

Glory in Scripture is fame, recognition, splendor, honor, majesty, or praise. When the bible talks about human glory, it is often closely linked to suffering and loss. For instance, we are "…heirs of God and fellow heirs with Christ, provided we suffer with him in order that we may also be glorified with him" (Romans 8:17, RSV).

Jesus, who left home, family, career and inheritance for Father's sake, will receive great glory and honor in heaven for what he suffered. It is the same for us. Jesus invites us to walk that journey together with him. As we share the experience of leaving things we love behind for a greater love, we will inherit with him the reward of glory in heaven.

And Father loves any sacrifice made for his son. In his generosity, even things you endured foolishly, where you missed the mark or went beyond what heaven asked of—even in your mistakes, the heart to leave things behind for Jesus will be honored in heaven.

1. *"Jesus, what is something I left behind for your sake that you really appreciated?"*

2. *"Jesus, how did it impact you to leave your home and family behind to follow your call?"*

3. *"What were you thinking when you smelled the sawdust of your carpenter's shop for the last time, and closed the door on that season of your life?"*

4. *"Sometimes what I've given up for you makes me feel like I am in last place in the race to get ahead in the world. What do you want to say to me there?"*

5. *"Jesus, tell me about the glory you will share with me in heaven."*

JOURNAL

GOODNESS

Matthew 20:25-28

"Jesus called them together and said, 'You know that the rulers of the Gentiles lord it over them, and their high officials exercise authority over them. Not so with you. Instead, whoever wants to become great among you must be your servant, and whoever wants to be first must be your slave—just as the Son of Man did not come to be serve, but to serve, and to give his life as a ransom for many.'"

While human society says that doing well looks like attaining wealth, status or positions of influence, Jesus turns status on its head. Status in heaven comes through service.

The Bible clearly records humanity's universal derision at the role of a servant. "The lowest of slaves he will be to his brothers," was the curse Noah gave Canaan. One could say that Noah introduced three social classes in his Genesis 9:25-27 pronouncements. When Isaac blessed Jacob he made him lord over his brother and stated that Esau would serve him.

Joseph's brothers were outraged when he shared a dream that implied they would have lower status and bow to him. We instinctively shrink back from taking on a servant role.

But from the beginning, God had a different dream about what a servant could be.

For instance, look at his conversation with a lonely, abused, and rejected maid—Sarah's low-class, foreign servant, Hagar (Genesis 16:7-13). He seeks her out in the wilderness, gives her specific directives, then he goes on to name her baby, foretell his gender, and give her a glimpse of her son's future. But he also tells her to return and submit to Sarai—not because Sarai was in the right, but because *Hagar's destiny would be fulfilled by accepting the role of a servant*. Father touches her desire to be seen and valued (afterward she called him "the God who sees") with something far beyond what she hoped for: her son would still inherit the promise to be a great nation, and she would be recognized as a forerunner of Jesus in accepting the role of a servant to reach a greater destiny.

In a culture that thought in terms of class and power, Jesus was constantly reaching out and serving those with no opportunities and no chance of paying him back. He did what he saw his father do with Hagar—just as her destiny came to fruition as she took on the role of a servant, Jesus accepted servanthood as the path to his call. And he lays out the same path for us: that our destiny is fulfilled as we take on the role of a servant.

In showing us the pleasure of God in servanthood, Jesus makes goodness, doing well and coming through for him accessible to every Christian, no matter what their role or position.

1. *"What does it give you, Jesus, when the oppressed are seen and served?"*

2. *"Father, what happens in your heart when I choose to lay down my life for others?"*

3. *"Father, what gift of service could I do that would make you happy today?"*

4. *"Jesus, the need of the crowds pressing around you was huge. I struggle with knowing how I can open myself to broken people's tremendous needs and not get overwhelmed. How did you do that?"*

5. *"Jesus, how do you want to come and serve me today?"*

JOURNAL

....

....

....

....

....

....

....

....

....

....

....

....

....

....

....

....

....

....

....

....

....

....

....

....

....

....

BEING KNOWN, LOVE

Matthew 20:30-34

"Two blind men were sitting by the roadside, and when they heard that Jesus was going by, they shouted, 'Lord, Son of David, have mercy on us!' The crowd rebuked them and told them to be quiet, but they shouted all the louder, 'Lord, Son of David, have mercy on us!' Jesus stopped and called them. 'What do you want me to do for you?' he asked. 'Lord,' they answered, 'we want our sight.' Jesus had compassion on them and touched their eyes. Immediately they received their sight and followed him." (NIV)

One interminable day when I was a teenager, I spent about eight hours blindfolded. I could barely see light, much less where I was stepping or if the peas were on the fork before it reached my mouth. Mostly, they weren't!

It was a sobering experience. Being blind, deaf, losing a limb, or even being lost, alone or sick (you name the need) can be a life-altering experience. Our fears rise up and assail our confidence and security, and we become reliant on those around us to offer guidance and help.

So, like these two blind men, we cry out, "Have mercy on me!" But sometimes instead of the help we need we encounter a cool disdain from the crowd. They avert their eyes, avoid meeting us or tell us to shut up and stop causing a ruckus. Where our desire is to be seen and known, we receive the cold shoulder of rejection.

But the One who was abandoned and rejected himself has great compassion toward us in our time of need (see Hebrews 4:6). The blind men sensed that someone of great grace was passing by. Even without the gift of sight, Jesus' magnetic presence drew them. Ignoring the naysayers, they shouted louder, "Lord! Son of David, have mercy on us!"

And he did.

Jesus halts, spins on his heels, and calls out to them with an amazing invitation: "What do you want me to do for you?" He *sees* them, he *knows* their need, and he *demonstrates* his love. And then he answers their request. With compassionate touch, they are made whole. Wow!

In the same way today, he sees your need and feels the compassionate love of someone who has been there himself. His question to you is, "What do you want me to do for you?"

1. *"Jesus, if you are asking, the desire I want you to touch for me is _____."*

2. *"Thanks for asking what I want and need—I am really grateful that you pay attention. Here's what it means to me that you ask..."*

3. *"You seem to take special pleasure in blessing the people the world ignores. Tell me about that part of you—I want to know more."*

4. *"Papa, I have a deep desire to know that you see me and love me right now. How have you been showing me that you see me this week?"*

5. *"The crowd didn't care about the blind men—they just wanted them to keep quiet. I've experienced that! Why do you want me to keep on asking even when I feel like a nuisance?"*

JOURNAL

FREEDOM, COMFORT

Matthew 21: 18-22

"Early in the morning, as he was on his way back to the city, he was hungry. Seeing a fig tree by the road, he went up to it but found nothing on it except leaves. Then he said to it, 'May you never bear fruit again!' Immediately the tree withered. When the disciples saw this, they were amazed. 'How did the fig tree wither so quickly?' they asked. Jesus replied, 'I tell you the truth, if you have faith and do not doubt, not only can you do what was done to the fig tree, but also you can say to this mountain, 'Go, throw yourself into the sea,' and it will be done. If you believe, you will receive whatever you ask for in prayer.'" (NIV)

After leaving their lodgings without breakfast that morning, Jesus and his disciples set out on the two-mile hike into the city of Jerusalem for the day. Down the road they spied a fig tree in full leaf, and Jesus turned toward it, hopeful that they might find a meal on the go. Some fig trees bear a small early fruit (either with or before the leaves), so the tree seemed to hold promise, even though early figs weren't particularly tasty. Jesus and his band stepped under the spreading tree, brushing their hands through the leaves… and, disappointingly, found nothing. Maybe the false advertising of a fruit tree with no fruit reminded Jesus of what he found in the temple the previous day.

The story of the cursed fig tree follows immediately after the triumphal entry into Jerusalem

(fruit!) and cleansing the Temple of a horde of price-gouging vendors and tourists doing their empty religious duty (no fruit!). He cursed the tree that bore no fruit, making the same point as when he cleansed the fruitless temple.

But how does this story speak to our desires? If religious rituals and empty devotions have left you feeling trapped, fruitless and hopeless, Jesus says, "That's not who I am! I came so that you could experience life and freedom in abundance. If you are trapped in a lifeless religious system, even inside my house, even if it is condoned by big-time national leaders, I will overthrow it to make room for you to meet the true me. Watch, and be amazed at how quickly I wither any religious clap-trap that doesn't bring us closer together."

Jesus is fiercely loyal to you, and loves to come through for you. He will not tolerate anyone robbing the two of you of your fellowship. He demanded that even the outer court of his house, the Court of the Gentiles, be a place of prayer, so that *all* people without exception could come to him. You are welcome in his house.

1. *"Jesus, what in my life are you causing to wither so that I can meet the real you?"*

2. *"Jesus, what piece of religious clap-trap do you want to set me free from today?"*

3. *"What image would help me understand how protective you are of our relationship?"*

4. *"Jesus, tell me again what I have to hope for. My hopes have gotten beaten down by life."*

5. *"Jesus, here's what it means to me to know that you are for me…"*

JOURNAL

HONOR, RECOGNITION

Matthew 23:8

"But you are not to be called rabbi, for you have one teacher, and you are all brethren. And call no man your father on earth, for you have one Father, who is in heaven. Neither be called masters, for you have one master, the Christ." (RSV)

It is so easy to forget our connection to our family in heaven, and buy into the idea that fame, status and position are the way to fill our deep desire to be recognized and celebrated. Have you ever caught yourself thinking something along these lines:

- *"If I were a real Christian I would be in ministry."*
- *"Pastors and missionaries have a special relationship with God that I don't have."*
- *"People should call me 'Pastor' or 'Reverend'—it's only right that they honor my position."*
- *"The people on the platform get more honor and recognition than me, and they deserve it."*

Jesus speaks to that emptiness with a command that is also a picture of heaven. There are to be no status symbols among Christians. No special titles. No larger-than-life figures who lead charmed lives, treated like kings and enjoying privileges the great majority don't.

"In heaven," Jesus is saying, "we don't treat each other like that. We are a family, and we relate like brothers and sisters, not like members of a social hierarchy. Each one of us is unique. Each is honored and celebrated for who he or she is, but all are equally loved by Papa. No one is less a son or more a daughter because of what they have or haven't accomplished—*every* son and *every* daughter is special to Father."

It is human nature to compare ourselves with one another and try to find our place in the hierarchy. We angle for titles, positions and accomplishments, even in the church, because they look like they will fill our deep desires to be known, to belong, to be special.

Jesus calls you to leave that sad pursuit behind and receive what you already have as a member of heaven's family. You are a sibling of Jesus, just as loved and celebrated by your Daddy as the greatest evangelist, prophet or saint. Paul and Peter are your brothers, Mary and Martha your very own sisters. You will stand together with them in heaven, not in the distant relationship of a fan and a movie star, but embracing, kissing and laughing for joy like family welcoming a dear brother or precious sister home from exile.

1. *"Daddy, how am I special to you today?"*

2. *Take a few moments and let these words sink into your heart: Jesus is your blood brother.*

3. *"Jesus, you aren't ashamed to call us brethren[5], so I guess I won't be either. So, bro, tell me something about what it means to be your brother or sister."*

4. *"Father, what do you want to honor in me today?"*

5. *"Daddy, sometimes I am afraid to believe I really belong in the way you say I do—I've been disappointed so often, and heaven can seem so far away. How do you want to touch me there?"*

---

5   Hebrews 2:11

JOURNAL

RECOGNITION AND REWARD

Matthew 23:11-12

"He who is greatest among you shall be your servant; whoever exalts himself will be humbled, and whoever humbles himself will be exalted."

I love God's reward system! Jesus told us to "make friends for yourselves by means of unrighteous mammon, so that when it fails they may receive you into the eternal habitations" (Luke 16:9, RSV). What he means is, if you use the stuff of this world to invest in and serve people, they will be there to cheer you when you enter into heaven.

Everything has its reward in heaven. If you receive a prophet, you will receive a prophet's reward. To put that in more contemporary terms, host the speaker in your home and you will get the same reward as the speaker. Set up chairs for the meeting, and you will have the same reward as those on the platform. Prepare lunch for someone serving Jesus and you will be rewarded just like them. Even giving a cup of cold water to a child won't be overlooked.[6]

This is why the greatest and most highly rewarded people in heaven will be those serving in secret in the background. While the leader of a ministry receives the reward of that particular ministry, the simple servant who helps many different people and ministries in practical ways gets the reward of all of them!

This is the same reason Jesus tells us to go into a windowless room and pray in secret, or to give without one hand knowing what the other is doing. Public ministry is rewarded in the here-and-now with affirmation, new opportunities and honor, but a simple task done without recognition, just for Jesus, will be gloriously recognized in heaven.

To exalt something is to lift it up, to publicly display and acclaim it as great. This verse says that will happen to you. Father's desire is to exalt you in heaven—to honor you publicly before the entire audience of heaven for what you have done for him. Even your smallest kindness will not escape notice. You will be cheered wildly by your peers, your spiritual heroes, the angels, your savior and bridegroom and your God.

1. *"Jesus, what have I done this week that means the most to you?"*

2. *"Father, why do you get such a kick out of recognizing the unrecognized, and rewarding those whom humanity looks down on?"*

3. *"What about me are you delighted in, that you are looking forward to displaying before all of heaven?"*

4. *"Jesus, how am I great in your eyes?"*

5. *"Jesus, I am a little embarrassed when I think about being cheered by all on the stage of heaven. What do you want to say to me about that?"*

---

6   If you'd like to study God's reward system, see Luke 16:1-12; Matthew 10:40-42, 6:1-21, 20:1-16; Luke 6:20-36; and Matthew 25:31-40.

....

....

....

....

....

....

....

....

....

....

....

....

....

....

....

....

....

....

....

....

....

....

....

....

....

....

....

....

....

LOVE, COMFORT

Matthew 23:37

"Jerusalem! Jerusalem! Murderer of prophets! Killer of the ones who brought you God's news! How often I've ached to embrace your children, the way a hen gathers her chicks under her wings, and you wouldn't let me." (MSG)

Have you ever felt a relationship was going down the tubes and tried desperately to keep from ending?

I remember working with another leader who was constantly doing things that injured me and others on his team. He was a good man with a great dream, and I didn't want our relationship to end. But I just couldn't endure the injustice of the situation any longer. I tried every way I could think of to get his attention. I pled, confronted, asked questions, showed him specific examples, confronted again. Nothing changed. To my great sorrow, I finally left.

That experience helps me understand who Jesus is. His chosen people, his bride-to-be, the ones he was prepared to die for, didn't want the relationship. The Greek word ethelesa (want) is the key to this passage. "How often I wanted (ethelesa) to gather your children together… and you were unwilling (ethelesate)." In other words, "I really wanted to be with you, but you didn't want me to."

The analogy Jesus uses offers a beautiful window into the depths of his desire for us. In times of danger, baby chicks scurry under the huge bulk of their mother and shelter in the warm, downy safety. Jesus aches to be that for you. He will gladly risk himself for you, encircle you with his big, strong arms and hold you tight. He loves seeing you run through the door when you are in trouble, so he can kiss the ouchy and make it alright.

This love is so big it can absorb every mistake, snub and tantrum you throw at it, and keep right on joyfully offering you refuge. "How often I wanted to gather you," means his desire to draw to his arms the rebellious, cantankerous Jerusalem-dwellers was constantly with him.

He desires you in that way. The only thing that can stop it is if you say, "Jesus, get out of my life." It's pretty hard to turn off Jesus' desire for you!

1. *"Jesus, tell me about your desire for me. How do you want to gather me to you today?"*

2. *"What do you like about being a mother hen to me?"*

3. *"Jesus, here's where I want to run to your shelter today: ____. How do you want to receive me?"*

4. *"Jesus, how'd you keep your love on when your own people kept abusing you and your friends?"*

5. *"Jesus, tell me about your arms. What are they like?"*

....
....
....
....
....
....
....
....
....
....
....
....
....
....
....
....
....
....
....
....
....
....
....
....
....
....
....

BELONGING

Matthew 24:31

"At that same moment, he'll dispatch his angels with a trumpet-blast summons, pulling in God's chosen from the four winds, from pole to pole." (MSG)

It was late in the day, and Jesus was resting on the Mount of Olives when the disciples came to him for an explanation of another of his strange sayings. A half-mile across the Kidron valley was the glowing Temple Mount. Nestled in the valley below, the Garden of Gethsemane was gradually swallowed by the lengthening shadows. Only three days before his death, Jesus may have pondered spending the last night of his life in that very garden.

The topic of the day seemed to be warnings, destruction and desolation. Jesus had poured cold water on their admiration of the incredible temple complex, saying that the beautiful buildings would end up as a pile of gravel. Confused, they sought him out to hear more about what to expect and how they would know when the world was ending.

He began by warning them not to miss the signs of the times; but seeing the fearful expression his apocalyptic words generated, Jesus decided to share his hope with his friends.

The message is, "Don't worry! When I come back, it'll be spectacular—you literally won't be able to miss it." Jesus draws a picture of messenger angels, an unmistakable trumpet call, signs in the sky and a gathering of his own from every compass point on earth. If the target is the heart, Jesus hits the mark spot-on, addressing our desires for freedom, joy, completion, and coming home to a place where we will belong.

We will not be abandoned, forgotten or miss out on that glory-day. Our longing for heaven echoes his.

1. *"I do long for that day! What will that be like for you when the trumpet sounds?"*

2. *"When have you seen my desire for heaven echo yours?"*

3. *"What are some things you are looking forward to when we are together?"*

4. *"In the middle of this struggle I'm facing, what hope would you like to give me for today?"*

5. *"So what is it like for you to anticipate all the good things you have dreamed up for us?"*

JOURNAL

TO COME THROUGH, LOVE

Matthew 24:45-47

"The trustworthy servant is the one whom the master puts in charge of all the servants of his household; it is the trustworthy servant who not only oversees all the work, but also ensures the servants are properly fed and cared for. And it is, of course, crucial that a servant who is given such responsibility performs his responsibility to his master's standards—so when the master returns he finds his trust has been rewarded. For then the master will put that good servant in charge of all his possessions." (Voice)

Many of us come from church cultures where we have been subtly indoctrinated into the same performance system Western culture works on. Steeped in this vantage point, it is easy for us to read this passage as an admonition to be good in order to get the Master's approval and get ahead—as though being trustworthy is something we *do*, not what we *are*.

But trust is fundamentally a relational word. It implies that someone else is able to count on you, because you care about what they care about.

Years ago I often did ropes courses with teams to develop trust. We would do "trust falls," where one person gets up on a ledge and falls backward into the arms of the team. It requires trust, because if they don't catch you, the landing is going to hurt!

In those moments you don't want people catching you who are trying do it right so others will like them or so they can be the hero. The only safety those folks are focused on is their own! You want someone who cares about your well-being, who will give it all to make sure you don't hit the ground and get injured.

This kind of trust is a way of *being*—*being* a caring person. When that's who you are, then coming through for others is the natural outgrowth of being you. No one will hand over all their possessions to someone who does all the right things to be noticed, or has malice in their heart, or is just competing to be the best. The trustworthy servant is one whose heart loves the things the Master loves.

Ultimately, we come through because we care. We feed the servants because we love them. We watch over the household needs because we love the Master, and it's his house.

Faithfulness without love is empty, and there is no wisdom in it—only an empty standard. But if we are faithful because we love, we are living from Father's heart. What a privilege! We get to care about what he cares about; and through this, even our most menial tasks change the world and bring in his kingdom.

1. *"Papa, tell me how you feel about how I've cared for what you care about."*

2. *"Jesus, you really came through for me, and I love you for it. How have I come through for you?"*

3. *"Papa, tell me what you value about the trust we have built in our relationship together."*

4. *"Let me bask in your love—go ahead and tell me again how much you love me!"*

5. *"Jesus, let's surprise someone today by speaking words of affirmation over their life. Who could we honor, and how can we make love real for them today?"*

JOURNAL

APPROVAL, TO COME THROUGH

Matthew 25:19-23

"After a long time the master of those servants returned and settled accounts with them. The man who had received the five talents brought the other five. 'Master,' he said, 'you entrusted me with five talents. See, I have gained five more.' His master replied, 'Well done, good and faithful servant! You have been faithful with a few things; I will put you in charge of many things. Come and share your master's happiness!' The many with two talents also came. 'Master,' he said, 'you entrusted me with two talents; see, I have gained two more.' Well done, good and faithful servant! 'You have been faithful with a few things; I will put you in charge of many things. Come and share your master's happiness!'"

Papa has entrusted us with responsibilities so that we can experience the joy of coming through for him. But when the master is gone for a long time, sometimes phenomenal hurdles can stand in our way!

Catherine Marshall LeSourd's life is a great example of facing this reality and coming through. After overcoming a serious illness, her husband suddenly died, and she found herself a single mother with a young, fatherless son to raise. It was 1949.

As she held onto the promise that "God causes all things to work together for good" (Romans 8:28), Father reminded her of her teenage desire to write. She sensed him saying, "Go forward and I'll open the doors before you."

Catherine took her dormant, twenty-year-old desire off the shelf and began to live it. Within six weeks of her husband's death, she was editing Peter Marshall's sermons for publication. In roughly a year, thousands were reading her first work, *Mr. Jones, Meet the Master*. She went on to edit and write ten more titles.

She found approval in hearing Father say, "Well done!" And then she sensed a new opportunity to come through: "Catherine, your job is to spread his message." Catherine continued to write, invest and spread the message, and eventually two of her works (including Christy, her mother's story) were made into movies.

Her husband had risen to the pinnacle of his profession as Chaplin to the U. S. Senate. But because she was willing to follow her desire to come through for Father, Catherine ended up leaving a larger legacy than her husband's.

Today, your life offers opportunities to come through for Father, just as Catherine Marshall did. What is it that's been entrusted to you? He has not given it to you as an opportunity for failure or to be punished if you do it wrong, but as an opportunity to succeed. Coming through means facing obstacles, and that can be difficult. But take heart—he is eagerly waiting to share the joy of his approving "well done!" with you!

1. *"What will it be like to be with you and to share in your happiness and approval?"*

2. *"Father, what do you want to say 'Well done!' in me today?"*

3. *"Jesus, who am I in this area of being trustworthy? What name would you give me?"*

4. *"How have you been touched when I've persevered through life's rough patches?"*

5. *"Papa, what do you experience in your heart when you see my faithfulness?"*

JOURNAL

SECURITY

Matthew 25:34-40

"Then the King will say to those on His right, 'Come, you who are blessed of My Father, inherit the kingdom prepared for you from the foundation of the world. For I was hungry, and you gave me something to eat; I was thirsty, and you gave me something to drink; I was a stranger, and you invited me in; naked, and you clothed me; I was sick, and you visited me; I was in prison, and you came to me.' Then the righteous will answer Him, 'Lord, when did we see you hungry, and feed you, or thirsty, and give you something to drink? And when did we see you a stranger, and invite you in, or naked, and clothe you? When did we see you sick, or in prison, and come to you?' The King will answer and say to them, 'Truly I say to you, to the extent that you did it to one of these brothers of mine, even the least of them, you did it to me.'"

In a way we don't usually notice, this passage speaks of your security in your relationship with Father and in his desire to bless you. Here, Jesus tells us that the reward we are to inherit was "prepared for you" by Father from the beginning, while the eternal punishment was *not* prepared for humans but for "the devil and his angels." Jesus wants you to know that it was not his will that any of us should perish. Those who go to punishment (to his sorrow) chose to live in the devil's kingdom rather than to give allegiance to the King.

There is no free will in the presence of God, other than for those who have already chosen him. His glory is so overwhelming that it overpowers any will that would resist it. As scripture says "Every knee shall bow and every tongue confess that Jesus Christ is Lord" (Philippians 2:11, see also Isaiah 45:23). Everyone will acknowledge his lordship, but not all will want it.

Free will is an irrevocable gift. Papa won't take it back by force, or compel the unwilling to live in his presence. Only the fully willing are free within the fullness of his presence.

Your life on earth is practice, a training ground where you learn to become fully willing. Every mundane situation where you act out of the heart of Jesus—like meeting people's physical needs for food and clothing, or their desire for companionship when sick—counts as a choice to lean into him. Simple service makes you more fully willing, and increases your readiness to joyfully embrace the irresistible glory of heaven.

Today, Jesus invites you to look back at your life and be secure. Ever sat at the bedside of a sick child, or cleaned up after someone you love vomited? That readies you for heaven. Have you donated clothing to Goodwill, or stopped by the roadside to change a flat? You are getting in shape for heaven. Ever visit someone in jail, take food to a neighbor after a birth or death in the family or even refill a dinner guest's glass? Every act of kindness is a choice to move toward Jesus; and each choice makes you more ready than ever for heaven!

1. *"Papa, tell me again how I am secure in you."*

2. *"Jesus, what's something I 'did unto you' recently that you appreciated?"*

3. *"Daddy, the idea that some people end up in hell bothers me. I know I won't always understand why you do what you do—but I trust you. Tell me—will it be alright?"*

4. *"Why did you give me free will, Jesus?"*

5. *"Show me one thing I've been doing lately that is good practice for heaven."*

JOURNAL

LOVE

Matthew 26:6-12

"Now when Jesus was at Bethany in the house of Simon the leper, a woman came up to him with an alabaster flask of very expensive ointment, and she poured it on his head, as he sat at table. But when the disciples saw it, they were indignant, saying, 'Why this waste? For this ointment might have been sold for a large sum, and given to the poor.' But Jesus, aware of this, said to them, 'Why do you trouble the woman? For she has done a beautiful thing to me. For you always have the poor with you, but you will not always have me. In pouring this ointment on my body she has done it to prepare me for burial.'" (RSV)

Jesus and his inner circle are ensconced at the table of Simon the leper, a stone's throw from Jerusalem. After a triumphant entry into the capital for the Passover feast, the cleansing of the nation's great house of worship and a series of amazing healings, it seemed like the sky was the limit.

In his moment of triumph, however, Jesus seems strangely subdued. A dark thread of suffering, disaster and the end of the world runs through all his stories. In person he seemed more... mortal, more introspective than in the past. Rather than embracing the exciting opportunities before him, he spoke repeatedly about his death.

But swept away by the admiration of the crowds, the disciples could only see the great destiny standing before them. Hadn't Jesus completely outmaneuvered the political and religious leadership? With the whole nation on their side, surely they were safe from even the Sadducees cunning? Newly aware of the political tug-of-war going on around them, the disciples saw only the political repercussions of Mary's act.

Couldn't Jesus see that taking expensive personal gifts and the luxuries of the rich was a giant no-no for a man-of-the-people like himself? The favor of the masses was won by taking the side of the poor, not perfuming himself up like a rich prostitute!

However, Jesus' mind was not on politics. As the house filled with the fragrance, he perceived that his Father had come, through this woman, to touch his heart and ready his body for burial. It was Father, saying, "Son, you are on the right track. I am with you in this, and I love you dearly. This will all be worth it." For Jesus, this was a God-moment of getting back in touch with the joy set before him that would carry him through the agony ahead.

"She has done a beautiful thing for me" is not just because of her sacrifice and devotion, but because in that moment she carried the heart of Father to a troubled son. Her story will always be told because she saw the pain of the Son of God, and touched his heart.

1. *"Jesus, what is a beautiful thing I have done to you?"*

2. *"Jesus, what is something I've done that others don't approve but you see as beautiful?"*

3. *"Jesus, what were you feeling in the moment Mary anointed you? What was going on in your heart?"*

4. *"Jesus, what beautiful thing have you done to me in the last week that I haven't recognized?"*

5. *"Father, how did it impact you when you saw Mary ministering to your son? When have you felt that way about me?"*

BELONGING, TO COME THROUGH

Matthew 26:26-29

"While they were eating, Jesus took some bread, and after a blessing, He broke it and gave it to the disciples, and said, 'Take, eat; this is My body.' And when He had taken a cup and given thanks, He gave it to them, saying, 'Drink from it, all of you; for this is My blood of the covenant, which is poured out for many for forgiveness of sins. But I say to you, I will not drink of this fruit of the vine from now on until that day when I drink it new with you in My Father's kingdom.'"

After practicing the familiar Passover ceremony from their youth, what they were experiencing with Jesus was a jarring departure from tradition. For one thing, they were having the meal a day early. That *never* happened! Then there was how Jesus edited the blessing. Normally, it was a ritual explanation of Israel's historic deliverance from Egypt. "Blessed art thou, O Lord our God, King of the universe, Creator of the fruit of the vine"—that was expected. But comparing the broken bread to his body and the wine to his own blood was a shocking addition.

To this point, Jesus' talk of his impending death may not have fully sunk in. But any remaining rationalizations of his imminent death were quickly brought to a halt. A broken body sounds violent. Blood poured out alludes to sacrifice.

After upsetting tradition and smashing his disciple's remaining illusions, he goes on to grab them with an amazing promise. He takes a vow of abstinence—"I'm swearing off wine from now on, until I can drink it with you in Father's kingdom."

Wine is the symbol of covenant and celebration. Jesus is saying, "There is no one else I will covenant with, no one I will celebrate union with, until we have the wedding party in heaven. I am committed to you."

He's made a commitment to wait for you, to come through for you. His words, "with you," are so inclusive, calling to your desire for fellowship and belonging. And it's an invitation to reunite in the glory of Father's Kingdom. Wow!

We have his approval. We have a personal, engraved invitation to be a part of that heaven-celebration with the disciples. In a grand and glorious Kingdom, our one-and-only, Jesus is waiting for us!

1. *"What do you want me to know about your pure delight in waiting for me?"*

2. *"You and Father are so generous! How do you see me reflecting your glory that way?"*

3. *"Jesus, give me a taste of the anticipation you have for our reunion in Father's Kingdom!"*

4. *"Jesus, tell me something I don't know about our future together. What will it be like?"*

5. *"Jesus, why did you take that vow of abstinence?"*

JOURNAL

COMFORT

Matthew 28:8-10

"The women, deep in wonder and full of joy, lost no time in leaving the tomb. They ran to tell the disciples. Then Jesus met them, stopping them in their tracks. 'Good morning!' he said. They fell to their knees, embraced his feet, and worshiped him. Jesus said, 'You're holding on to me for dear life! Don't be frightened like that. Go tell my brothers that they are to go to Galilee, and that I'll meet them there.'" (MSG)

Two solitary women headed out the city gate just after sunrise, bound for the tombs. Only a few days before, they had endured their leader's betrayal by a close friend, by their nation's leaders and finally by the whole Jewish people, who shouted for the release of a hardened criminal instead of their Messiah. The man they'd placed their hopes in was tortured to death under the cruel hands of the Roman occupiers. While watching his last agonized breaths, the ground shook in a terrifying earthquake, strong enough to damage the massive temple.

After a Sabbath filled with shock, grief and fear, the women had wiped away tears to head for the cemetery, anxiety growing at every step. Would the guards still be there? What further curses, harassment or worse must they endure to say a final goodbye to their Jesus? In their fear and uncertainty, a deep desire for comfort rose in them.

Suddenly, the earth swayed again in a rumbling aftershock, knocking them to the ground. A searing brightness strobe-lit the scene, petrifying the guards: an angel! And then he spoke directly to their desire: "Don't be afraid: Jesus is risen! Here, take a look!"

The tomb was empty. By turns amazed, joyful, in shock and trembling, the women struggled to absorb that wild swing from abject grief to soaring hope. Taking a moment to gather themselves, they stumbled off to tell the disciples—and ran smack into Jesus himself.

"Good morning," he said, as if this was like any other day they'd met on the sidewalk. When they fell dazed at his feet he touched their desire again, adding, "Don't be afraid."

Now, I'm probably going to need to hear those words a few times if I am in those women's shoes! After witnessing a brutal execution, two earthquakes, an angelic visitation and a friend raised from the dead, I'd need something to steady myself.

I imagine there was a hint of a smile on his lips when Jesus breathed, "Good morning!" As in, "I can't wait to see the look on Mary's face when she realizes it's me!" That's Jesus, having a little fun delivering the best news they've ever heard. Then he continues as if nothing out-of-the-ordinary had happened: "Tell the bros to head up to Galilee and we'll get together there. See—it's all turning out fine, just like I told you it would."

Sometimes the best cure for anxiety is to see Jesus wink at it. Nothing lightens a mood like having the one who descended into hell and came out laughing (instead of being traumatized) say, "You're on the ride of your life now, aren't you, baby?"

1. *"Jesus, what are you laughing with me about today?"*

2. *"I'm anxious about ____ today. What does that look like from the viewpoint of heaven?"*

3. *"Jesus, let me experience a little piece of that fountain of joy you carry this morning."*

4. *"What's the joke of the day, Jesus?"*

5. *"Jesus, I deeply desire comfort sometimes. Tell me again how everything is going to be alright."*

JOURNAL

ADDITIONAL RESOURCES
FOR TOUCHING DESIRES

Here are a few of the additional resources for meeting God in your deepest desires available through the bookstore at www.Meta-Formation.com.

- *Desire Discovery Card Deck* by Tony Stoltzfus
  A set of conversation cards to help you identify core desires and the emotions that spring from them.

- *The Calling Journey* by Tony Stoltzfus
  Create a calling time-line to understand how to meet God in suffering and how he has been using all your life circumstances to move you toward your destiny.

- Soaking Music by Julie True (various albums)
  Spontaneous, meditative worship that helps you soak in the presence of God.

- *Revelations of Divine Love* by Juliana of Norwich
  A 14th-century mystic touches the heart of Jesus in amazing ways.

- *Dialogue with God* by Mark Virkler
  A practical, widely-praised guide to developing a conversational prayer life.

Training in Working with Desires

If you long for deeper transparency, relational depth and heart change in your leadership sphere, the Leadership MetaFormation Institute has the tools and training you need. Founded by Tony Stoltzfus, LMI has three key objectives:

1. **Personal Transformation**
   A rich, personal experience of heart engaging through encountering God in one's deepest desires;

2. **Tools to Transform Others**
   We provide coaching tools to help leaders walk others through heart transformation;

3. **Building Transformational Cultures**
   LMI offers tools and practices for building organizational cultures where heart transformation is the common experience.

Each of LMI's three courses includes an intensive, three and one half days workshop based around an innovative, highly-experiential learning style. Using everything from learning games, the arts, original music, theatrical staging, relational teams and more, LMI creates powerful God-encounters that immerse you in the ways of the heart. This is not a typical, talking-head seminar: you'll get live practice and experience with every skill and concept that is taught.

LMI training is designed for ministry leaders, business owners, pastors, managers, helping professionals (such as counselors and coaches)—any leader who wants to walk others through deep change or build a culture of transformation.

For more information, visit LMI's website at www.Meta-Formation.com or contact them at Office@Meta-Formation.com.

DESIRE
INDEX

The meditations that touch on each particular desire are listed below: